Praise for *Make it Happen*

'Campaigning is an incredible force for good – it has the power to improve people's lives. So, if you're a young person who has an idea and wants to change the world, read this book and help make it happen.'

Sadiq Khan, Mayor of London

'Inspiring and practical. An indispensable handbook to changing the world.'

Caroline Criado Perez OBE, author of *Invisible Women*

'A personal, powerful, passionate, pragmatic, punchy book from one of Britain's most exciting Gen Z activists. A great guide to moving and shaking with joy, spirit and real world results.'
Deborah Frances-White, creator and author of *The Guilty Feminist*

'Amika George is a credit to her generation and makes me feel so much better about the future. Her tireless campaigning to make period poverty a thing of the past in the UK has helped millions of girls, the social and economic benefits of this will be seen for many years to come. I'm delighted to see that she has put her passion into words.'

June Sarpong OBE, broadcaster and presenter

'Amika George is one of my favourite people on earth – she embodies why the world is so excited for generation Z! *Make it Happen* is an inclusive, powerful, political, intelligent and *brilliant* book about how one person can truly make a difference in this world. If you feel remotely fed up with the status quo, you need this book in your life!'

Scarlett Curtis, writer and activist

'Amika is an inspiration to us all and a personal hero of mine.'
Josie Naughton, co-founder of Help Refugees

'I wish I'd had this book when I googled "how do you change a law" at the beginning of my fight to make upskirting illegal. I would have felt so supported and understood what being an activist really takes. Can we get this book on all school shelves?!'
Gina Martin, campaigner and activist

'This is a mad world. A world struggling through a period of grave, existential crisis. Amika and her book, *Make it Happen*, is the ray of light we all need to make sense of this world. To set things right. To catalyse change, to leave no one behind.'
Trisha Shetty, activist and founder of Shesays

MAKE IT HAPPEN

MAKE IT HAPPEN

HOW TO BE AN ACTIVIST

AMIKA GEORGE

ONE PLACE. MANY STORIES

HQ
An imprint of HarperCollins*Publishers* Ltd
1 London Bridge Street
London SE1 9GF

www.harpercollins.co.uk

HarperCollins*Publishers*
1st Floor, Watermarque Building, Ringsend Road
Dublin 4, Ireland

This edition 2021

1
First published in Great Britain by
HQ, an imprint of HarperCollins*Publishers* Ltd 2021

HB ISBN: 978-0-00-837760-1
TPB ISBN: 978-0-00-843435-9

Typesetting in Kalix by Palimpsest Book Production Limited,
Falkirk, Stirlingshire

Printed and bound in Great Britain by CPI Group (UK) Ltd,
Croydon CR0 4YY

To Appachan

CONTENTS

INTRODUCTION

Spring 2017

I was at the kitchen table, having breakfast before school, scrolling on my phone. 'Girls Too Poor to Buy Sanitary Products Missing School' was one of the top stories on BBC News.*

I was curious; the byline declared that a charity supplying pads to girls in Africa had been asked to divert their supplies to the UK. I clicked on the link, intrigued. The article described how the charity Freedom4Girls had been contacted by a school in Leeds after teachers started noticing some girls' patterns of

---

* It is important to note that trans men and boys, non-binary people, and gender non-conforming people menstruate too, and many women and girls do not. I initially had a very limited awareness or understanding of this when I started campaigning against period poverty. As a result, I underestimated the importance of inclusive language in my campaigning and activism. I now work to ensure that my activism is as inclusive and intersectional as possible by using the terms 'students' or 'children' to describe those in need of access to period products and to be more inclusive of trans and non-binary experiences of menstruation. The articles I describe above, however, which prompted me to start Free Periods, only described the plight of cisgender girls missing school, which is why I have used the term 'girls' here and in other similar contexts.

absence. These girls, who lived in England, girls just like me, couldn't afford to buy pads or tampons. Many of them came from families that were struggling to put food on the table. The journalist interviewed teenage girls who admitted that they would often go to school with wads of tissue paper wrapped around their underwear, hoping it would keep them dry until the end of the day. They would miss school for days every month, not wanting to risk bleeding all over their uniform. One said she was too scared to tell anyone, keeping it a secret until she finally worked up the courage to ask for help months later. Another said she was overwhelmed when she started her period. She had no idea what was happening to her body and started missing school every month. She felt isolated and alone.

I sat back in my chair and thought about what I'd just read. I was outraged. Like many of us, I'd heard about girls being too poor to afford period protection in other countries around the world. In fact, just weeks earlier, I'd read an article in *Time* magazine about period poverty in India, and the impact on a girl's life when she drops out of education. I remember the sadness I felt reading how, in the country in which my grandparents had grown up, 113 million girls between 12 and 14 years old were at risk of dropping out of school simply because they weren't equipped to manage their period due to the shame and stigma of menstruation. Some schools, especially those in rural areas, didn't provide toilets that were safe and hygienic, with access to running water and the means to dispose of pads safely. I remember shuddering as I read about how girls used leaves, hoping they would absorb the blood. *Leaves.* I hadn't been able to get my head around it. School just wasn't a place for a poor girl with a period.

When my grandma came over that evening, I spoke to her about the article. I wanted to know what it had been like for her, when she was growing up in India. She laughed at the shock on my face when she told me how she would fashion her own pads from neatly folded cloth inserted into a belt, which she would hoist onto her hips in the days before disposable products were common. We spoke about the shame, so culturally embedded in a country where menstruation is considered unclean and impure.

But this felt different. This article in front of me was about girls in England. In what was one of the most prosperous countries on Earth, crippling poverty meant that girls were missing out on the education to which they were entitled. The British Government is routinely praised for upholding human rights and supporting those in need, but the injustice of students in the UK being unable to get an education because of their period stunned me. No matter how I looked at it, the injustice was overwhelming; why should periods hold anyone back from going to school, from realising their potential, and achieving their dreams?

It's not fair that anyone should be at a disadvantage simply because of their biology. How can we even come close to achieving gender equality if one of our basic needs isn't being acknowledged and met? And how could it be that no help was being offered to those who weren't able to manage their period? It was as if society was dismissing them; saying they didn't matter.

Until that point, I had never thought about how it would feel not to have a pad or tampon when I needed one. I'd never thought about it because I was lucky enough to have a bedside drawer stocked with a few packs on standby every month. I knew how unsettling and stressful it was to start a period in class and find I didn't have a tampon in my bag, but I'd usually ask a friend, and there was always someone with a spare pad or tampon in their locker or rucksack. There was always a short-term fix, and when I'd get home from school, there would be as many as I needed. But how many times could these pupils keep asking their friends for pads before it became clear that this wasn't a one-off, before they'd have to admit that they couldn't afford the cost of their period? I searched 'period poverty in the UK' and was taken aback to see that there were several reports online about girls using newspaper, old T-shirts, or socks stuffed with toilet roll as makeshift pads, just so they could go to school. That was the only alternative.

The first time I got my period, I was at school. I was 10. A few months before, I'd gone to a café with my mum and, over slices of cake, she'd told me that my period might arrive any day. We talked about how she'd started hers at a similar age, while playing in the sand on a family holiday in France. The signs that I'd be starting mine soon were most definitely there. But it arrived sooner than expected.

At primary school, after a music lesson, a boy in my class tapped me on the shoulder and told me quietly that there was blood dripping down my leg. I felt sick with embarrassment as I glanced down and saw a neat line of fresh blood working its way along my calf. I panicked: I'd started my period and had no idea what to do.

As I looked up, I could see him laughing, a crowd of boys looming just behind, peering over him to have a look. Every face in the class turned towards me. 'I've cut my leg,' I said quietly, my voice shaking with false calm. I walked slowly out of the room to the nurse's office in case any movement might increase the flow. It was humiliating, and as soon as the nurse walked into the room, I started to cry. She was kind and wrapped an arm around my shoulder, but it was clear she didn't want to mention the subject of menstruation. Instead, she called my mum and sent me home early that day, as if I'd come down with a temperature or a nasty bug. I was confused.

I was the first of all my primary school friends to start their period, and, crushed by that first experience, kept it to myself. Many periods passed, and the entrenched shame and stigma surrounding periods only became increasingly evident as I got older.

Sitting at the kitchen table that morning, I read and reread the article about girls missing school, and began to understand why staying at home was the preferable option for most of them. Why put yourself through all of that – the laughing, the ridicule, the shame – when it was far easier to skip school and be close to a bathroom?

To me, it was quite clear: if these girls were being held back because of their period, if they were subject to regular gaps in their learning, this could affect the entire trajectory of their lives. The consequences would be far-reaching. It would affect their ability to take part in their education (particularly compared to their male peers), get a job, and pull themselves out of poverty. Period poverty was perpetuating a vicious cycle of deprivation for these girls, possibly for generations.

When I was 15, in the months approaching my GCSE exams, I was struck down with a bad case of the flu and had to take some time off school. As I lay in bed, day after day, gradually recuperating, I remember being gripped by a rising panic as I thought about the schoolwork I was missing and the volume of reading and catching up I'd have to do to compensate. When I returned to school, I was met with a long list of chapters to teach myself, essays to hand in, and upcoming exams to prepare for. I felt overwhelmed. Everyone had moved on, while lessons made far less sense to me as I'd missed chunks from previous classes.

Now I wondered how it would feel to experience that feeling month on month, year on year, knowing that others were at an advantage. I imagined being one of the girls I'd read about who had to make a single pad last all day. How would I have been able to concentrate in class, knowing that it might leak onto my skirt? If it were me, I might even give up going to school at all, knowing it was just no use, that I was never going to be fully present in all my classes.

It wasn't fair, and as the days passed, I found myself getting angrier.

It seemed that everyone was condemning period poverty. There were reams of investigative reports and news stories over the next few days about the rise of period poverty and child poverty in the UK. Teachers admitted packing pads into their bags for those who 'forgot' to bring in period products. Parents confessed to stealing pads and tampons for their children from pharmacies.

A few weeks after these reports were published, the media fell silent and it wasn't reported again. It appeared that the story had come and gone and that nothing was going to be done by the UK Government to help these girls.

That's when I started the Free Periods movement. I spent three years fighting for free period products to be available in English schools. Today, that's a reality. No child in England needs to miss school because they are too poor to have a period.

My journey was disjointed – sometimes unplanned, sometimes strategic, sometimes chaotic. There were highs that left me feeling the happiest I've ever been, and lows where I would sit on the floor of my bedroom in tears, wondering what on earth I was doing. I kept diaries, notes, jotted down things to do and never do again! Free Periods started as an online petition, but it soon morphed into an unstoppable, global movement. It fills me with so much joy that every day, I'm contacted by young people from around the world who are inspired to do more to make change, who are taking control of their power, harnessing their collective anger to question and disrupt the status quo, and fearlessly standing up for the causes they care about. Whenever someone contacts me asking me for help in their own activism, I tell them about my experiences, caveating everything with: 'This is so hard, but you have to do it anyway!'

Campaigners and activists, globally, are reclaiming politics as something that belongs to us. We are proving that everyday people with normal lives, people like you and me, have the agency to affect the most remarkable change. With traditional politics feeling increasingly distant from our daily reality, with so many politicians failing to look, sound or live like us, we're taking matters into our own hands. The nature of politics is changing, and so is the future of activism, protest, and disruption.

What I've learnt is this: anyone – absolutely anyone – can be an activist. This book will help you to find your inner voice, the one that's been lying low, unsure of whether it should be allowed out, or the one you never knew you had.

And today, more than ever, we need people like you to stand up for change. It's a strange and troubling world we live in now. I don't think I've ever felt so uneasy about what lies ahead for my friends and myself. It seems as though only certain voices are being heard, and maybe you feel that way too. Politics appears to be a narrow sphere dominated by a small group of privileged, white men. This is the powerful, homogenous elite who have the authority to make decisions about society and the precious things that affect our lives every single day. We are bombarded by reports of people in power making decisions that seem completely wrong-headed or, worse, indefensible. We gasp in collective horror. A week later, it's yesterday's news and there doesn't appear to be any way of holding those people in power to account. People like you and me have to refuse to let those things lie. In this weird, frantic, and somewhat apocalyptic political and social climate, has there ever been a better time to stand up for change? Isn't this the perfect time to jump from a place of safety and try to create something better?

The United Nations enshrines equal rights in its charter. But why, out of 191 heads of state, are there only 13 women? Extreme inequality is spiralling out of control, and the human cost is devastating, particularly for women and girls. Across the globe, the work of women is consistently undervalued. Worldwide, figures show women do 75 per cent of the work, receive 10 per cent of the pay, and own just 1 per cent of property. Almost half of humanity is living on less than $5.50 a day, while the power and fortunes of those who recline comfortably at the very top of the economic pyramid (predominantly men) are protected by their avoidance of, as much as 30 per cent, of their tax liability. In fact, men own 50 per cent more of the world's wealth than women, and the world's 22 richest men enjoy more wealth than all the women in Africa.

Whatever you decide to do, don't wait for that watershed moment, for someone else to come in and present the perfect solution. I waited – and nothing happened. Don't think for one second that there's someone else out there who cares about something more than you do, and is better placed to do something about it. Perhaps, in deciding to take a stand against the injustice that weighs heavy on you, you will be the person who changes not just your life, but the life of others. Discover the enormous untapped power and impact of your voice and don't listen when you are told that everything is fixed, unquestionable, and inevitable. Your actions will show them that they are wrong. And by being bold enough to get going, you'll encourage others to stand up, too. A community of passionate changemakers will rise around you, inspired by your conviction, and will not back down when they are dismissed or demonised. All you need to do is choose to get started. For every movement or uprising, there has been a person who, like you, has decided that it was time for urgent and compelling change, who hesitated about starting, who started and then stumbled, but who fought on.

That's why I've written this guide, including everything I learnt from Free Periods. It's the book I wish I'd had before I started out and it will show you that *you* can be the orchestrator of change. Use it however you see fit. Let it serve as a guide to dip in and out of, or keep it alongside you in your activism.

Let's do it. Let's not wait. Let's start marching and make it happen. Let's reclaim our voice and power. And let's not stop.

CHAPTER 1

CHOOSE YOUR CAUSE

Whatever kind of person you are, you can be an activist. I believe that activism comes in many forms. Refuse to be typecast as a do-gooder or hippie tree-hugger, and know that incredible change has been achieved by a whole range of people who couldn't be more different from each other. I don't believe you need to be the most outgoing person in your community, or the most eloquent speaker, or ultra-resilient and resourceful to do this. You can be any sort of person.

I'm not the loudest person in the room. Neither am I the most confident. If you'd told me four years ago I would be speaking in front of TV cameras, or that I'd be standing alone on an open stage holding a mic on the other side of the world, I wouldn't have believed you. But the urge to act takes over, and you feel you just have to do it. That feeling comes from something which really, really matters to you. Whatever you want to change, whatever issue you feel is demanding to be heard, it can be you who makes it happen.

Our world is a scary place right now. As I write this, I'm reading about impending wars across nations, where diplomacy seems to be wearing thin, and political leaders tweet about solutions in the form of destruction and retaliation. I'm reading about the consequences and terror of a global pandemic killing thousands and plunging the world into collective despair. I'm reading that a worldwide economic downturn is looming, and that mass unemployment, deprivation, and even famine could cause so many more to suffer.

I'm reading about a climate crisis so severe that raging bush-fires have forced thousands to flee their homes, and floods and storms are the biggest killer in countries already crippled by desperate levels of poverty. I despair that my future will be foreclosed by politicians who say we can't afford to tackle the climate emergency. Politicians who are careless about our future because they may not live to see the consequences.

I'm reading about misogynistic, racist, and divisive comments made by world leaders, which no longer elicit widespread outrage and condemnation, purely because we've become inured to them. When there seems to be no hope for the world, it's easy to become apathetic and, instead of feeling angry, find ourselves accepting.

But the world is full of people refusing to give in to despair, and against all odds are growing and cultivating seedlings of hope and change. We are getting bolder and bolder in seeking out spaces where we can make sure we are heard, and we're using the internet and social media to expand our reach and connect with others who share our concerns and determination to change the status quo.

You may have been propelled to action because you're directly affected, or you might have become aware of an injustice that's staring you in the face and refusing to move away. Whatever the reason, remember you have power – and use it.

Listening to that feeling inside which nudges your conscience, asking you to do something, anything, is often the hardest part of getting going. That feeling is easy to ignore if you try hard enough, but don't ignore it. Be open to it, and let it do its thing.

I've heard the negative, internal voice that tells us we are all insignificant, and nothing we can do will ever make a real difference. It says: 'What do you think someone like you can do to change something so big?' or 'You're going to look stupid if you have a go and it doesn't work out.' I've heard that voice tell me I'm not good enough, not brave enough, not old enough, not white enough, not the right kind of person to make a difference.

I'm glad I didn't listen to that voice, because it was only when I started to act that it slowly but surely died away, until it was barely a whisper – and one I could ignore.

Similarly, when you're confronted with injustice, hypocrisy, or blatant double standards, don't ever let yourself feel that it's just the way it has to be, because *nothing* is ever the way it has to be. No matter how rigid or entrenched something appears to be, I really do believe that things are always in a state of flux, and it's for us to grab control of the wheel, start the debate, and steer the conversation in the direction we want it to go. Don't squeeze yourself into the mould (wrong shape, wrong size) that society claims you need to fit in order to be worthy of attention. It suits some, but not all. Create your own and make it look exactly as you want it to look (the shape that fits you, the size that fits you).

Why should we let those in power, who don't look like us, speak like us, or know what matters to us dictate how we ought to live? What the hell do they know about the issues that hit us hard? They don't want you to challenge or disrupt. Why should they? I am so fed up of hearing young people being called Generation Snowflake, a flippant term created to diminish and undermine us. Apparently, we're too busy pouting and editing our selfies to care about shaping our world.

It's far easier for people in power if everybody tows the line, eyes down, lips pursed, and hands behind backs. Everything – from books to advertising, films and TV – informs us that power looks, sounds, and feels a certain way. We've bought into that for generations, haven't we? But as Wael Ghomin, the activist who helped spark the 2011 Egypt uprisings, affirms in his book *Revolution 2.0*, 'the power of the people is so much stronger than the people in power'. And we, as ordinary people, hold more power than we fully understand.

Think about the kind of society you want to live in. Is it one where everything is predetermined and prescribed, where we wait patiently in line for our paltry slice of the pie, and then find out it tastes pretty horrible when we get it, wait in line again and go back for more? No. So think about the situation and consider how many people a particular issue affects, aside from you (if it's one that affects you directly), and whether anything is likely to change if you make the decision to ignore it.

Caroline Criado Perez is a true heroine – a proper, indomitable, feminist powerhouse. She waged a brilliant and inspiring campaign to force the Bank of England to put a woman on an English banknote, and also fought for a statue of suffragette Millicent Fawcett to be erected in Parliament Square in London. She's unstoppable and fearless. I asked her what advice she has for someone who's itching to do something impactful but doesn't know where to start. She told me:

Choose something you can't help campaigning on. Campaigning is tough. It's exhausting, it takes over your life, it's often thankless, and there is no set endpoint. You keep going till you win. That could take weeks, months, or years: many suffragists fought their entire lives for women to have the right to vote. Many of them died without seeing success. So you have to make sure that you can keep going. And the only way to make sure you can keep going is if you literally can't stop yourself. That's how you know you have the right campaign on your hands.

Caroline didn't consider herself a feminist at all growing up. She admitted to being a teenager who looked down on women, and thought men were better.

Then suddenly, in my mid-twenties, I had my mind changed by a book called *Feminism and Linguistic Theory*. In particular, a section on the use of the generic male in grammar – so 'he' to mean 'he or she', 'man' to mean 'humankind'. Like a lot of people who don't know much about feminism, I'd heard that feminists object to this usage – and, like a lot of people who don't know much about feminism, I had been used to rolling my eyes at it. Here was a perfect example of how ridiculous feminism was – and a perfect opportunity to show how much more logical I was than other women. Because, unlike those irrational creatures, I understood that 'he' meant 'he or she' and that everyone knew that. 'Who cares?' I thought. These petty trivialities don't concern me.

But then I read the next sentence. The author cited studies that show that when women read or hear these words, they picture a man. And that made me pause. In fact, it blew my mind. Because I realised, for the first time, that I was picturing men when I heard these words. And I just couldn't believe that I had never noticed it before. After all, as a woman, shouldn't I be picturing women for these supposedly gender-neutral words – at least 50 per cent of the time? How had it taken so long – and having it pointed out to me – for me to notice?

Caroline started to realise just how filled with men her uncon- scious mind was. Because it wasn't just these generic male words that conjured up men in her head. It was also words that had a far greater claim to gender neutrality: words like lawyer, doctor, professor, writer, journalist, scientist. All of these words conjured up an image of a man.

> I couldn't help connecting this preponderance of men in my head with the extremely low opinion I had always had of women. After all, what did I really know about women? I know now how much women have been written out of our history. I know about the art, the literature, the scientific discoveries made by women and attributed to men: their husbands, their supervisors. But back then? My history lessons had been full of men. The 'great' literature I was told to read was almost exclusively by and about men. Scientific progress was presented to me as the work of men. Was it any wonder I saw my sex as an obstacle to be overcome in my quest to be seen as fully human?

She admits:

> I started to get really angry at how my sex had been misrep- resented to me – and the impact that had had on me growing up. All this pressure I felt to show I wasn't 'like other girls', just so I had half a chance of being treated like a human being. The impact it had had on my self-confidence. I felt it wasn't right that this carried on happening to girls. And so when I came across examples of how we represent the world as almost exclusively male, of how the people we celebrate in history are almost exclusively male, I felt I had to challenge it. Because I knew from personal experience the impact that can have.

Also, more practically, this is the kind of change a person on her own can effect. There are huge and far more intractable injustices that require years and whole organisations working on them to solve. But a banknote? Yeah, I could do that.

Starting small

When I was just months into starting my campaign, Catherine who, like me, was 17, got in touch. She told me that she'd been feeling really low and sometimes guilty about the state of our world and all the injustices in it. She felt powerless to make change and asked me whether my activism gave me some form of reprieve, a feeling of empowerment in a world that seemed to have lost its way and was moving further and further away from her.

Catherine and I began chatting over email, and she told me that she'd suffered from mental health issues and had just moved out of her family home. She felt she needed a cause to fight for, to give her some hope and purpose, to bring her back.

I know things weren't easy for Catherine. She had everything working against her, telling her not to try. But she resisted that pull to sit back. She started campaigning for better training for GPs at her surgery on mental health issues. She found her spirit and drive and this, in turn, gave her a feeling of optimism about her future, a hope that things could be better.

She was incredible in helping me raise awareness about period poverty and, at the time of the Free Periods protest, even though she wasn't able to afford the journey to London, she worked hard, tweeting and posting about the protest, asking everyone to share and be there. Activism found Catherine, and it's stayed with her.

I know how easy it is to think that issues are too big to tackle, to stand back and look at an issue that's hitting you hard and feel turmoil, that it's much bigger than you. To believe this is just the way things are. That can put you in a place of despair and powerlessness, which is hard to rise above. It's easy to think that you can't be the one to change things, either. Not when you feel like *everything* is already a struggle.

Catherine started small. She approached her own GP practice, asking what she could do to get the help she needed, and started questioning the current systems in place. She tells me:

> The biggest thing I get from activism is a sense of connection and belonging with people and the world around me. As someone who feels isolated, it helps a lot that I can talk to other people who feel the same as I do about an issue and figure out a way to do something about it together. It's definitely empowering. No one else is going to do it for us. It's still hard for me, and other people my age, to feel like we deserve a voice because a lot of the time people don't listen to us. That's why we need to listen to and lift each other up. We need to take control because there are people in positions of power that are making decisions about our future without asking us, but it will, ultimately, fall on us to deal with the consequences.

Catherine's journey into activism, fighting to address issues that affected her directly at a micro level, show that absolutely anyone can fix systems that are broken, and that sitting up and demanding something is done is the very first step to change. There is no one demographic that holds the key to creating change. For Catherine, it was about resolving her own frustrations with the system, but in doing that, coming to the realisation that her life could have a wider impact and benefit other people, giving her purpose. She drew strength from knowing that she was making things better for everyone; caring for others and showing empathy for them can liberate us.

I met Shiden Tekle at a photoshoot to celebrate youth activism. Shiden and his friends became so frustrated at the lack of Black actors in TV and film that they began to recreate iconic film posters, such as *Titanic*, the Harry Potter franchise, and *Skyfall*, with Black actors shown in the lead roles instead.

Shiden was angry that Black faces were often just token additions in mainly all-white castings. He tells me:

> I've been racially abused since I was 12. We are always looking at the media and never seeing any positive representations of Black people. In big films, Black characters are often playing criminals and drug dealers, and that quickly conditions people to believe that all Black people are like that. So, we decided to put Black faces in the big movies, and challenge people's perceptions and assumptions.

Shiden and his friends had created the posters, featuring their friends and family, for their own bedrooms and social media accounts, but their posters hit the headlines across the UK and were soon splashed across billboards in his local area. And a movement, Legally Black, was started, which drove debate and discussion around the issue of racial misrepresentation in the media.

> I didn't ever think it was going to get as much coverage as it did. But once we got that coverage, we were able to push for the things we wanted to achieve, such as initiating the discussion about anti-Blackness in the media with commissioners from UK broadcasting companies and the impact of negative depictions of Black people, especially on young people. Changing things in the media is difficult, but it can

be accomplished and I have learnt a lot about who has the power and how to use traction gained from campaigns to accomplish future goals.

As a campaign group, we have always said that we do not advocate for the removal of white characters and the insertion of Black characters. We say Black people should be given agency and control of their narratives. This is happening a lot more now, but racial stereotyping is still a prominent issue throughout the media, both on screen and off. We also try to be inclusive in the language we use by addressing how the media affects other racial communities too. However, we choose not to speak on behalf of other communities because we can only speak to our own experiences.

I ask Shiden about how someone gets started in their mission to change something they care about:

You don't need a complex, well thought-out plan of how you'll defeat structural injustice to make a difference and become an activist. It can be as simple as coming together with a bunch of friends and deciding to do one act around a cause, such as, for example, using art to create a message about a social issue. That's how, in time, unequal power structures are dismantled, one pillar at a time. When I got into activism, I was lucky enough to have people around me who supported us, such as the Advocacy Academy (an organisation that supports young activists in South London) and other people we connected with through Legally Black, which showed me that having a good relationship with your community is essential if you want to make a difference.

Shiden tells me that maintaining the same level of commitment throughout his activism hasn't been at all easy. He was constantly getting burnt out.

> Having to balance a lot of things, including Legally Black, can be a lot sometimes, but when I care about things, I persevere. Also, as a young person, you're not always taken seriously by people who want to work with you – but as the years go on, we were able to create a safe space for our ideas and ensure we weren't overworking ourselves.

So, you've decided you have to do something about our world, and you're reading this book to get started. What you need next is to decide what to do. Whether you're tackling an injustice at a grassroots level, or you want to create change on a global scale, all activism starts with a decision and a first step, and from there, *you* decide how big you want to go. Whether it's small-scale activism or a worldwide campaign, this book will show you that the core principles are exactly the same.

Let's look at micro campaigns at a local level: all around us, we are faced with so much inequality and injustice that it can feel suffocating. Many issues are left unchallenged; they exist and become more deeply embedded. Sometimes, they can be so normalised and commonplace that we stop seeing them as an injustice. Our brains block them out.

When my extended family, made up of my grandparents, aunts, uncles and cousins, get together for dinners, I notice that it's always the women milling about in the kitchen. The men huff and puff about politics and the state of the world while they recline on the sofa, and my mum, aunties, and grandmother bring endless, steaming pots of food to the table, and scurry back to the stove. It's the way things are in our family, partly culturally entrenched, and, until recently, I didn't even question how sexist it was. It was almost as though I didn't see it. That's just how it's always been. I've been pressing my brother to do something about it, and although he laughs and does his best to irritate me by telling me that a woman's place is in the kitchen, I've noticed that he now does go into the kitchen to help. The only boy in a room whirling around with women.

Find your power

We're too humble. We don't often see our strengths and the power that lies in us. We don't realise how much we can do with what we have. Real strength and courage lie in deciding to be the one who stands up and fixes it. But getting started is the hardest part. As aviation pioneer Amelia Earhart once said, 'The most difficult thing is the decision to act, the rest is merely tenacity.'

I suggest listing all the things you're good at. Every single one. Don't leave anything out. If this feels like a challenge, imagine you're writing about a friend, rather than yourself. (We're much more generous to our friends than we are to ourselves!)

Here are some of mine: I'm organised. My life is planned via a series of Post-it notes and detailed lists on my phone, navigating me throughout the day and the week. I'm empathetic. I'm compassionate. I'm loyal. I'm opinionated. I'm strong. I'm stubborn. I don't like giving up.

Now list your skills. Are you artistic? Are you good at writing? Are you methodical? Do you like motivating people? List them all down. Even if you can think of only a few strengths or skills, don't worry! As you go on your activist journey, you will start developing skills you never knew you had. And as you go forward

and do things you've never done before with passion and reso-
lution, your confidence and sense of purpose will grow.

Supermodel and true activist Adwoa Aboah founded Gurls Talk
– a safe, judgement-free online and offline community, which aims
to destigmatise mental health and encourage open conversation
about body image, sexuality, self-care, and more. It's the organisation she wishes she'd had as a young person battling mental health
issues and addiction. She explains how she used her power to make
a difference, and the challenges she faced when first getting started.

When my activist journey began, I had to sit with myself for
some time and dig deep to conjure the confidence. Truthfully,
I didn't know where to start. I didn't know what Gurls Talk
was going to become, but I knew I had to make a difference.
And although that was scary, that's where the excitement lay,
in not knowing and putting myself out there for the first
time. I never imagined my personal story was going to translate into something like Gurls Talk – I didn't realise it was
going to bring together such a strong-minded community
who were really looking for something like this.

Every single one of us has our own story and experience
that can make a difference, and that's where the power is.
Nobody else can tell your story better than you. When I came
out of the other end of my recovery, I had such a profound
yearning to do something with all the knowledge I had been
given and I understood my story was bigger than me. I felt
if I could translate it into a movement, I could really effect
some change in the arena of mental health.

I met Nicola Mendelsohn, Vice-President for Facebook in
Europe, the Middle East, and Africa, in March 2020, at an
event for International Women's Day. She's a real force in the

industry, and is using her influence for positive change, speaking out about inequality and the need to narrow the gender pay gap in the tech industry. In November 2016, at the age of 45, she was diagnosed with follicular lymphoma, an incurable blood cancer. She tells me, 'Getting cancer does make you take a long hard look at your life and think about what you want to change.'

When I ask her about what she's learnt from her career, and what advice she has for young women, she tells me about the importance of being bold, open, and kind.

> Being bold is about not being afraid of speaking up. In my early career, I often knew the answers but would sit quietly in meetings. Then I'd get annoyed that someone else – usually a man – would answer. I've learnt how important it is to speak up and be heard and I try and encourage the women around me to do the same. Being open is about being prepared to try new things and new approaches. At Facebook, we have this great saying: 'What would you do if you weren't afraid?' It's so important to be prepared to try new ways of doing things without feeling like you can't because you're afraid it won't work. Being kind is pretty self-explanatory. In particular, COVID-19 has really taught us the importance of supporting each other and being kind. When you're in a leadership position, you do need to be prepared to give honest feedback but you can do so in a kind way.

Create your campaign

Choosing the issue that you want to tackle is difficult. Maybe you know exactly what you want to achieve, which is why you're reading this book. But just having the will to demand something different is a great place to start.

We are wading through injustices every day. Racism, misogyny, all kinds of bigotry and prejudice. The list is as long as it is depressing. We know that for centuries, people have been fighting for improvements in their communities, looking for alternative solutions, building up local groups and networks as a response to feeling invisible to those who wield the power. When politicians and leaders appear to stand with their backs to us, hands over their ears, we must force them to turn around, face us, and listen.

I'd often feel stunned when reading articles about injustices in society, but there was never any reason for me to even consider trying to attempt to fix the problem. Every issue seemed far too big, every inequality already so deeply entrenched, that I wouldn't even know where to start. The problem never seemed like it was mine to fix. When you read the news, the issues always seem to reflect a rigid and structural problem with our world, but these seemingly mammoth political issues, when broken down to a local level, suddenly become a lot more manageable and easier to connect with. The problem becomes more tangible – and, incidentally, this is where you have the most power to effect change.

Think of these kind of deep, structural injustices as tall buildings. You need to chip away at them brick by brick. As each brick falls, you're dismantling the rigid structure, until eventually, the bricks lie in a pile of rubble. Dislodging one, or a small number of bricks, is the key to getting started. You need to address those smaller issues within the big, broad issues if you want to make a tangible change. It's about fighting for the smaller wins to get the big prize. It's about winning hearts and minds on the ground first. The action of each person is crucial to the collective work being done across the globe.

Maya and Gemma Tutton are sisters. They started the

campaign Our Streets Now after they became victims of public sexual harassment (PSH) as schoolgirls. Gemma was only 11 years old when she was subjected to crude sexual remarks about her body by passing strangers on her way home from school. Gemma's experience is shared by over two-thirds of girls in the UK. The sisters decided they'd had enough of this misogyny and sexism, which is still unpunishable by law. Their campaign calls for all forms of public sexual harassment to be made illegal.

Maya Tutton tells me about what made them want to take action:

> As a society, we have normalised the harassment women and girls face while in public. As victims of PSH ourselves, and as an older sister who has witnessed its impact on my younger sister, we know first-hand the effect of this form of gender-based violence. I care about so many other injustices, but in a sense, all issues of inequality and injustice are interlinked – we work to challenge ableism, fatphobia, homophobia, and racism within and through our work, highlighting the importance of an intersectional lens when working to end PSH.
>
> If you don't know where to start, find others who do. I don't think we utilise enough those people who've gotten existing campaigns off the ground. I've lost count of the number of people who have helped spread Our Streets Now's message. Our early followers are the absolute backbone of our campaign, and have shaped how we work to end public sexual harassment. Writing to your MP about abortion pill provision during COVID, fundraising for cash-strapped women's organisations, or volunteering in a local shelter can profoundly change the world. It's not always about the 'big' actions, it can be a consistent desire to help those around you that makes the real difference.

Go as narrow and specific as you can in finding your cause. The danger of going too broad is that the campaign could easily lose focus, resonate differently with different people, and split your core support base. What you need is a single and stream-lined issue, which isn't so open-ended that it can be open to interpretation. Sometimes I'm asked whether campaigning to end period poverty is like sticking a plaster over an issue that stems from the wider, and more prolific issue, of poverty. My answer is this: as a teenager, how was I ever going to stamp out poverty when the causes are so far-reaching, complex, and systemic? What I *could* do was address a small part of it. For me, that was period poverty, an issue affecting thousands of students. It was an issue for which there appeared to be a solu-tion that was within touching distance, which *I* could play a part in delivering, so long as I had enough support from those who could make it happen.

Micro-activism and grassroots campaigns can take so many different forms. Working to solve issues that confront you every day in your own surroundings – the issues you live and breathe – means you're giving your community and cause a voice, and this can feel much more doable than going too large. Here are some ideas on how you can start flexing your activist muscles!

- Why not start researching issues in your area? Are local libraries on the brink of closing because of a lack of funds? Could you start looking into lobbying for funding from your local council? What about homelessness in your area? Could you persuade local businesses to provide one meal a day to a homeless person in their neighbourhood? Mental health issues in young people are on the rise, but is your school or workplace doing enough? Why not organise wellbeing days once or twice a year, where you get to talk about issues that affect your mental health every day, and work through solutions? We organised these at my school: for a week each term we'd have lunchtime sessions for yoga, mindfulness, silent discos, talks about the importance of sleep, and 'chocolate meditation'. It takes someone to get it off the ground, so why not you? Could you campaign for every person in your class, or school, to link up with a charity for the elderly and write to a pensioner who has no family?

• Why not ask your work or school to invest in reusable cups for each employee or student, or lobby for reduced food waste in your university canteen? Perhaps you could start a Green Team at your school or office to think of new ways of working to conserve energy, or to persuade curators of public buildings in your area to provide free water dispensers. You could campaign in your local area to ask every local business to sponsor the planting of a tree in your neighbourhood.

• Is there enough disabled access in your town or city? Could you lobby for local organisations to donate to local foodbanks in your area? Or campaign to get supermarkets to give food to the local soup kitchen every day?

• In the last 25 years, landfill has increased by 50 per cent since fast fashion became the norm. If you're fighting to change the perception of fast fashion either locally at school or work, or on a wider societal level, maybe think about practical measures that make it easier for people to change their habits as well as perception. Why not lobby for big stores to send boxes with free postage to people to enable them recycle their clothes? Or encourage local fashion chains to stock more 'pre-loved' clothes? Or organise fashion shows showcasing vintage fashion at your school or college?

- What about being an agent of change for gender equality by raising awareness of sexual violence in your area, or gathering a group of friends to stand up against street harassment? Or, if your school or college doesn't already have one, start a 'FemSoc' or local branch of UN Women UK.

If you want to elicit change, and you have the passion, the belief, and the hope, then do it. Yes, you can wait for someone else to lead that change, but why not you? Recognising the injustice, or the existence of a problem, and badly wanting to solve it is the crucial step, but understanding that the person to do it can be you is what will push you forward.

If you're struggling to figure out how to get started and whether you can do this, start by finding organisations and groups in your local area which are already fighting the good fight. It's a far less daunting method of activist action, and you might find that once you've gone along to a few meetings, you'll find sub-issues that you want to tackle separately. Plus, you've already made connections with like-minded people! Search for local volunteering or advocacy groups, or find out more about local centres that give talks and hold meetings on issues that you care about.

Remember that changes at a local level can benefit entire communities, and it just needs someone like you to see the change through. Local activism is like spreading your roots where you're planted. It's no longer a tangential sideshow to the business of politics. It's an essential counterweight, and it brings about real change, even if that change takes place beneath the surface, out of the spotlight.

I chat to Deborah Frances-White, the creator and host of The Guilty Feminist, the hit podcast with over 75 million downloads so far. She also happens to be a clever, sassy, and fearless stand-up comedian, author, and screenwriter. Deborah tells me about her three-pronged approach to making a difference.

Firstly, start with your passion. What keeps you awake at night? What injustice drives you wild with fury? What do you believe should be done? Are you furious about the way refugees are treated? That women aren't protected by legislation from upskirting? That tampons are a luxury item? Speak out on what you cannot stay silent about. Your intention and engagement will shine through and your conviction will change minds and engender action. You're far more likely to sustain a campaign if your heart is right in it.

Secondly, start locally. Who do you know who needs help? Is there a library closing in your area that you want to fight for? Is there a lack of advocacy for marginalised groups in your neighbourhood? Is there an injustice in your school or university, or an opportunity for positive and valuable representation? Do something local by talking to other residents, students, or colleagues and starting a conversation about what's happening in your 'hood. Lockdown, in a COVID-19 world, has created new local connections and your activism can use them to make a positive change in your part of the world.

Finally, start small. If you feel like the world is screwed and you're too small to help, start with one mini action to see how it feels. Go to the Amnesty website, find a cause that speaks to you, sign the petition, or click the link that sends a letter to the right person. Think it doesn't do anything? Think again.

Governments are often embarrassed into making changes because they see the world is watching and the cost of abusing human rights becomes too high for them. Send that petition along to one other person and invite them personally to sign it. If you have no money, amplify and ask people who do to donate to a cause. Follow a small movement, charity, or organisation that might be feeling overshadowed by world events and encourage others to do so. It'll give them a renewed boost to find they have fifty new followers. Do one small thing well. Then do another small thing well.

I remember standing in a refugee camp watching a small child eating a hot meal, and thinking of the person who donated the £2, the person who cut the vegetables, the person who stirred the pot, and the person who dished it up with a smile. I realised then, while the refugee crisis can seem overwhelming because governments won't take responsibility, lots and lots of small actions from us can have a huge impact.

Deborah tells me that she believes this is the end of an epoch:

Consuming and doing, doing, doing doesn't work. We need to learn how to be together and make room for each other if the human race is to have a future on this planet. This is our time to ask if the changes imposed upon us contain any lessons for us.

Activism is a demand for respect, equality, and autonomy. Feminism demands control over our bodies, representation, and legislation. During the pandemic and the lockdown, we've lost control over how many times a day we can leave the house and whether we can hug our mums or see our friends right now. Small things we took for granted. So it feels like a request for more control is futile. But it isn't. The system doesn't work. Lockdown is making its own case for that. It's time to step up and cocreate a world we do want to live in. This is an opportunity, not an excuse for inaction.

Activism has changed Deborah's life, given her purpose, and made her realise she can do a lot more heavy lifting than she ever imagined possible:

> I understand this now from my time building the podcast and meeting some super-sharp activists, movers, and shakers: the very definition of influence is the power to shift things a little off the course they'd have run without you. As Reni Eddo-Lodge says when asked how white people can be better allies to Black people – work out where you have power. Can you convince your parents to do something? That's power. Could you get better representation in your school for a marginalised group if you made your voice heard? That's change. Could you put an important topic on the agenda of a group you belong to? That's influence and influence is power. Now what will you do with that power? Working out where my influence is and using it to build networks of others who'll get online as an army or actually leave the house and head out to Calais to a refugee camp, that's incredible. That's a privilege. That's purpose.

The Global Goals

Now it's time to decide what you want to achieve through your campaign. If you need inspiration, look to the United Nation's 17 Sustainable Development Goals, also known as the Global Goals. If you already have your activism goals, see if one of them connects to one of the Global Goals. I bet it does!

These Goals are a universal call to action to improve the lives of everyone, everywhere. In 2015, they were adopted by every single United Nation member state (that's 193 countries) and a pledge was made to spend the next fifteen years ushering in ambitious action to deliver them by 2030. The Goals include Zero Hunger, Clean Water and Sanitation, Gender Equality, Quality Education, and Decent Work and Economic Growth.

I've tried to amplify the Goals, where possible, through my campaign. Ending period poverty is just one part of a bigger, global ambition to achieve gender equality (Goal 5) and ensure quality education for all (Goal 4).

I'm part of the Youth Power Panel, a group of twelve young people from across the globe, working to accelerate change and bring youth activists together in support of the Goals. One of the Panel members, Inés Yábar, a Peruvian sustainability activist, tells me how she's used the Goals to bolster her activism.

For me, the Global Goals are a way to quantify the quality of life we want to have in the present and the future as humanity. Although they have been set for 2030, we won't reach them if we don't start now. It's up to us to make these goals happen. For young people, it's especially important because we are acting now for the future we want to live in.

If we don't raise our voices, the people who make the decisions now might not take our interests into account. I believe in the power of each person to create a change, it's up to us to decide what change we want to bring about and work to make that happen.

Inés tells me how the Global Goals act as a frame for her activism. She was always passionate about working to alleviate poverty and reverse climate change:

33

For many, humanitarian work and ecology don't always go hand in hand. However, with the Global Goals, we can see that they're all interlinked because they are all part of a more sustainable future. To have sustainable cities (Goal 11) we need to have a society where inequalities are reduced (Goal 10), as well as responsible consumption and production (Goal 12).

I particularly like Goal 17, Partnership for the Goals. These goals have given me confidence in what I'm doing, because they've helped me understand how every action, no matter how insignificant it may seem, fits into a wider framework. When you decide to tackle one issue that you care deeply about, it can seem overwhelming, but knowing that what I'm doing fits in with the Global Goals, I'm reassured that many other individuals and organisations are striving for the same thing. One of our missions is ocean conservation. When some studies indicate that by 2050 there will be more plastic than fish in the sea, this might seem like a lost cause. But with the Goals we can unite with other movements that are working for the same thing and make a stronger impact together.

Bruna Elias, Lebanese architect and another activist on the Youth Power Panel, tells me how she's campaigned since 2016 to integrate the work and aims of businesses in Lebanon with the Global Goals:

The Global Goals can help to connect business strategies with global priorities. Companies can use them as an over-arching framework to shape, steer, communicate, and report their strategies, goals, and activities, allowing them to capitalise on a range of benefits. The Global Goals have been the North Star of all the projects and initiatives I have been working on, leading to many opportunities to solve challenges through business innovation and collaboration.

But Bruna believes young people hold the key to achieving the Goals by 2030:

Youth activism has played a major role in raising awareness on a wide spectrum of sustainable development topics such as poverty, health, education, climate change, inequality, and more. Their individual and collective efforts are central to the achievement of the 2030 agenda and averting the threats and challenges of today's world. Young people are demonstrating their continued leadership in their communities and countries. It is time to build on their calls to action to ensure that we have strategies for measuring the progress of the 2030 Agenda. Young people's insights, energy, and innovations are indispensable to the achievement of this collective vision.

Youth are among the most active in global responses. From helping in the small neighbourhood where they live to being on the frontlines and creating advocacy campaigns, young activists are doing so much. Their approach of activism is not mechanistic; it has become organic, as every student, researcher, innovator, and communicator can deliver on the Global Goals using their knowledge and skills.

Education plays a vital role in transforming our societies towards a sustainable future. Education empowers youth to face the complex and key challenges of the twenty-first century, enabling change and building better communities. As the world grapples with unprecedented challenges posed by the COVID-19 pandemic, I knew I had to use my activism and help my community. This is why I launched Lebanon

Learn, an online platform that collects unused laptops and donates them to students in need to enable them to continue their education at a distance.

When she was a child, Inés was taught by her parents to make rubbish bags out of newspaper to avoid using plastic. Different influences in her life helped to cultivate a sense of wider responsibility.

At church, I was taught to take care of others regardless of social class. At university, we managed to make *Ecosia* (a search engine that uses ad revenue to plant trees) the students' main search engine . . . all these things did not require me to attend a protest or talk about politics, but they shaped me to into the activist I am today.

So, where to start? Start where you are today with small actions at home or school. You'd be surprised at the impact you have. Also, I would say you are never too young or too old to start. I started becoming involved in consciously making a difference when I was 15, when many people still looked at me as a child without much to say. I've also met people who chose to become activists when they were retired.

The best time to start is today.

Finally, I would say it's easier than ever to be an activist today because there are so many causes to support and so many organizations that have paved the way. Many times, our role models seem like they are too put together, doing so much. But just remember that they too started somewhere.

Remember that while different countries tackle the Goals at a national level, you can do the same right where you live, where you can see the impact of change with your own eyes. Focus your campaign in your community, in your school or at work, and root yourself in one of these Goals and the specific targets within them. How incredible to know that what you're doing on the ground fits into this huge, global mission that every country is working towards to make our world better for everyone.

Can you persuade your school or workplace to sign up to a pledge to tackle one of the Goals? I was lucky enough to be on a small judging panel for a competition to find which school across the world had done the best work towards them. It was organised by The World's Largest Lesson, an exciting initiative to ensure that every child in the world grows up knowing and caring about the Global Goals and feels inspired to take action to help achieve them. So far, this initiative has reached millions of children in over 100 countries, which is amazing.

From reading through their entries and watching videos they had filmed of their work, I learnt that you can make the smallest of changes in your own environment and that this can ripple across towns, regions, and countries. The projects that stuck with me included a school in Uganda growing its own food for the kitchen to cook for students' lunches, and a school in Malaysia campaigning for positive body image through educational workshops for students. Check out the World's Largest Lesson's resources online, which are hugely inspiring and include videos written by and featuring activists like Emma Watson, Malala Yousafzai, and Serena Williams.

Every single thing you're met with that sits uneasily with you, that has you seething with indignation or starts to crawl under your skin, is a brilliant and untapped opportunity for change. Absolutely nothing has to stay a certain way forever, and it's all about deciding that the time for change is now and that the person to make that change is you.

There are always 100 reasons why you shouldn't get involved, but imagine if the world's greatest activists and changemakers had waited for someone else instead? Imagine if Rosa Parks had never sat down on that bus, or if Malala Yousafzai had decided that speaking up for girls' education was just too controversial, or if Gloria Steinem had wanted a quiet life. Imagine if they hadn't fought. Imagine if they'd waited for someone else.

Know your stuff

Now that you've chosen what you want to change, it's time to arm yourself with an arsenal of information that will help you to move forward.

You need to research your issue inside out and really understand the context of the injustice. Start digging to understand what you don't know. While doing this, keep asking yourself questions about why it exists, why nothing's been done, how much other people know about it, and who cares about it as much as you do. These questions are important in getting to really understand your topic in depth and thinking ahead.

It sounds like a daunting task, but don't let it put you off getting started. Here's a problem that you want to fix, and to do that, you want to be absorbing as much information as you can lay your hands on to be in a place where you can lift off and know you're absolutely ready to go! Of course, you will carry on learning and discovering new things as you go, and your learning should never stop, but at this stage, your aim is to fill your brain with as much information about your issue as you can. You're going to be the authority on it, and you need to equip yourself with a rigorous understanding.

Whether you're tackling a local issue or going big, read,

explore, and question. Greedily consume every article, every blog, every analysis out there, keeping a note of the ones that resonate with you. Keep thinking about how you can weave your voice into the existing narrative. I created a folder and saved every article I found useful, and slowly started building up a databank of facts and figures.

When I started researching period poverty, I couldn't quite believe how much information was out there. I felt overwhelmed. There were sometimes contradictory statistics. I took my time, and approached it like a mini-project, breaking down the research to make it less intimidating. I started with period poverty in the UK, then moved on to see what was happening with the issue in other countries.

I couldn't stop reading.

The more I read, the more I knew I had to do something. I felt angry and I felt let down. Here are some facts that really moved me and propelled me to act. I kept statistics like this to hand when discussing the problems with someone new, as they really illustrate the appalling consequences of period poverty:

- In Nepal and Afghanistan, 30 per cent of girls miss school during their period.*
- Almost a quarter of girls in India drop out of school when they start menstruating and the ones that remain miss, on average, five days a month.
- 20 per cent of girls in Sierra Leone miss school when they have their period.

* The research quoted here, carried out by the United Nations Population Fund, examined the experiences of cisgender women and girls.

- Only 45 per cent of schools in the least developed countries have basic toilets; in Nigeria there is one toilet for every 600 students. No wonder going to school when she's on her period is not an option for a Nigerian girl.

I read how the cost of these girls being excluded from education was as far-reaching as it was devastating. When girls drop out of school, they abruptly limit their potential to thrive emotionally, physically, and financially. Without an education, they're unable to lift themselves and their families out of poverty, but the consequences run far deeper. A girl who is forced to leave school is more likely to be a victim of child marriage (also known as child abuse), early childbirth, and domestic abuse. I was stunned to discover that in sub-Saharan Africa, a girl with no education is five times more likely to marry before she turns 18 than a girl with a secondary education.

I read about the culture of shame bound up in menstruation, the belief in some countries that when a girl has her period, she is impure. The stigma and shame were destroying lives and families. In Nepal, women were dying from being banished outside to a period hut in the bitterly cold climate, suffocating from inhaling the toxic smoke of the fire they lit to keep themselves warm, or suffering fatal snake bites. I read of the myths and superstitions surrounding menstruation, which are so deeply ingrained in certain countries that some women can't even bring themselves to say the word or are too embarrassed to buy pads. I couldn't believe what I was reading. Periods are a fact of life, affecting half of the world's population at some time or another, something that shows us that our bodies are working beautifully, allowing us to create new life. It was clear that on top of everything else, reframing menstruation in society's eyes was desperately needed.

The more I read, the more I knew this was something I had to do. As a 17-year-old girl who was able to go to school and access the period products I needed, wasn't I in an extraordinarily privileged position? Shouldn't I help those who weren't? I knew that in England the situation was far less damaging, but, as Plan International UK found, one in ten girls were known to be missing school due to period poverty. By refusing to do anything about it, weren't we, in effect, writing them off? Weren't we saying they didn't matter? That we didn't care?

I read a blog post by the author Kia Abdullah, who'd spoken out about how period poverty had affected her life every month growing up. In an effort to educate myself about what it was like to live in that fear, I contacted Kia, who told me that every month would bring a strangling dread. She started her period at 13, and for three years she didn't have access to pads or tampons. It was only when she was 16 that she got a job and bought her first pad.

She had a routine when she started her period. She took a roll of kitchen towel, ripped off two or three sheets, and then folded these in half. Folding the first set lengthways in her knickers, she laid the second widthways. She then had a total of twelve sheets worth of absorbency. This would last her two hours at most. Kia said that she often leaked into her underwear. 'Each month brought a weeklong prayer that I wouldn't stain my clothes.' At the time, she tells me,

I just got on with life because I didn't have an alternative, but I look back now and my heart aches for the girl I used to be. The truth is that I felt a deep embarrassment about my situation, which is why I never confided in anyone. Those who suffer from period poverty face not just a practical challenge (sourcing alternative sanitary wear, having to change more frequently, secretly washing stained underwear), but also pay a mental cost: the persistent fear of leaking, the fear of being 'found out', embarrassment about what they're having to resort to. It's a significant mental burden.

Kia couldn't bring herself to speak to anyone about not being able to afford menstrual products, despite having older sisters and a close circle of friends at school. She found it difficult because she had to contend with a double stigma:

At home, we never discussed periods or anything to do with reproduction, as it was taboo. At school, I was reluctant to admit to not having enough money. I attended an inner-London school and though my friends and I were on equal footing, I felt mortified by the prospect of admitting that I could not afford tampons or sanitary towels. The stigma around periods is powerful on its own; combined with poverty, it feels unbroachable.

Kia was sure that other girls she knew were also struggling to afford period products. She grew up in Tower Hamlets, which has the highest rate of child poverty in the UK. 'Poverty, coupled with cultural taboos around menstruation, surely meant that I was not the only one suffering.'

There had been plenty of comments under all the articles I'd read that questioned why families couldn't afford pads and tampons if they could be bought cheaply, sometimes for less than a pound. I put this to Kia, who tells me:

Many people with privilege believe that their graft, grit, smarts, and wit got them to where they are and find it very hard to acknowledge that wealth, class, luck, and privilege played an immeasurable part. Because of this, they find it hard to empa-thise with poor people or to understand that some people genuinely cannot afford a product that 'only costs a quid'. I would ask that they approach this from a place of empathy and to believe the young women – some of them still children – who say they need help. They're not saying it for fun or because they would rather spend their quid on a can of Coke. They're saying it because they're suffering.

I read about the work that was being done to help those suffering from period poverty, and made a list of all the charities and organisations working in different ways to help. I started searching online for people who had spoken out about it before, especially politicians, and saw that Baroness Burt had raised the issue in the House of Lords. I made a note to connect with her.

There are some key things it's worth prioritising as you do your research, and I've listed them here. You'll discover that knowing the answers to these questions will be hugely helpful in getting your voice heard and making a difference:

- Why do you think this issue exists?
- Are there any other people, groups, or campaigns that already exist in this area? Does it intersect with the issue you have in mind? Has anyone else tried to do the same thing? (If they have and it hasn't worked, why not? Can you go about it differently?)
- Are there any key people, particularly those in the public eye, who have spoken about it? Whose names keep coming up in conversations around it? Can you contact them?
- Has there been any coverage in the media? Can you gauge public opinion? Are people sympathetic or is the issue divisive? If so, why?

- Who wouldn't want you to achieve your goals? For example, are there businesses making money from the current situation? Could there be any cultural or societal reasons why it exists, or is it simply that no one else has tried addressing the issue before?
- Have any other schools, companies, cities, or countries done anything about this?

Don't let the amount of information put you off. Every article, piece of research, data, or statistic you find is there to help you. It's not an exam, so don't feel like you need to know or understand everything at once. You don't! This process will help you, in time, to really understand the issue so you can think and plan, and arm yourself with brilliant knowledge.

If you're making a change at a local level, there may not be masses of information available on the internet, but don't despair! Get together as much as you can. You might need to contact your local council or ask for some help to find out more.

I made a list of other activists who had worked in the same space and researched what they had achieved and asked them about the kind of challenges confronting them. Laura Coryton is a heroine of mine, and her campaign to abolish the tax on pads and tampons has directly led to the British Government pledging that the levy will be scrapped at the end of 2020. I reached out to her and she couldn't have been more helpful in encouraging me to get started.

When Laura was in her second year of university, her friend Verity sent her a *BuzzFeed* article about all the ridiculous things that are subject to sales tax. When she spotted tampons were listed, she was initially confused:

I thought: 'Maybe everything else is taxed more?', but the more I looked into the tax system, the more annoyed I became. I found that we don't pay tax on items deemed to be 'essential', including maintaining private helicopters, horse meat, and alcoholic sugar jellies, and that we do pay tax on 'luxuries', which include all period products from menstrual cups to tampons. Sound fair? I didn't think so either! That's when I started the petition. I honestly never thought it would be a popular petition when I started it. I just thought it would be fun and a good way to tackle this strange taboo about periods that impacts so many lives. I still can't believe the response the petition got! It makes me feel really motivated about the changes we can all make.

Laura agrees that anyone and everyone can be an activist. Particularly with the rise of social media, those who have never been able to have a voice finally have a platform and they cannot be ignored. 'We are seeing the rise of an increasingly diverse range of activists, offering new perspectives and solutions to age-old problems. We're getting things done. That's really exciting!'

Laura has made campaigning look deceptively easy. The truth is, she has faced some tough times.

'Sadly, most female activists receive pretty ruthless backlash. Trolls online have questioned how many journalists I have slept with to secure the publication of articles on tampon tax (as if running a petition signed by 300,000 people isn't enough); they have said I should "shut up and get back in the kitchen", that I'm a "poisonous witch" and a "hot piece of chicken".'

The first time she was targeted by a trolling attack, she was numb with shock:

I knew trolling happened but I always assumed it would never happen to me. It makes you feel this weird mix of embarrassment, shame, and vulnerability. I thought about stopping my campaign, until I realised something. I noticed that most trolls attacked me with the same sexist catcalling most women face on a daily basis. Only trolls actually document what they say. They record their own sexism, which only legitimises the acts of feminist campaigners. They're literally shooting themselves in the ... keyboard? That thought motivated me and from now on, I celebrate trolls for legitimising my activism and that of all feminists around the world.

When I ask Laura about whether she's found it difficult talking about periods when they are so stigmatised, her response is unwavering:

I actually find the way the period taboo has changed really quite funny. When I started my petition, my granny, for example, would always tell her friends, 'Laura is starting a petition on something but I'm not sure what' when she absolutely did know, as I would talk about tampon tax 24/7. Now, she won't stop talking to her friends about periods! It's fab. Similarly, when I contacted my local MP Mel Stride the same week I started the petition, he wrote back to me about four months later, saying it wasn't his concern. Now he's talking about tampon tax in the chamber as if he's always been the petition's biggest fan! Don't get me wrong, the period taboo is still thriving throughout society and it is something we all need to speak up about, but the amount of positive change we've seen in such a short space of time is so encouraging. It proves we can end period stigma. Period!

Who holds the power?

Next, we want to think about who – which person, group or organisation – has the power to accelerate a solution to your issue. Whose shoulder do you need to tap? Who needs to turn around and pay attention to what you're saying? Whose mind are you trying to change? It may be your line manager at work, your head teacher at school, your local MP, or the CEO of a large organisation.

When I decided to campaign for schoolchildren in England to be given free period products, I knew that the issue of period poverty in schools lay at the intersection of education, health, women's rights, and other socio-economic issues. At first, I was confused about who would tackle the problem. It definitely wasn't up to teachers to try to provide period products to those who needed them. Schools simply wouldn't have the funds in their overstretched budgets to provide pads or tampons for free. I figured that to give every child an equal footing in school, the solution would have to come from whoever held the purse strings in government. My instincts told me that it should be the Minister for Education, but I wasn't too sure. It could have been the Prime Minister, but I thought it best to target someone with a more specific role. I did some searches on the internet and read some articles to identify the responsibilities of the Minister of Education. It seemed that school budgets would fall under her remit, so I decided she would be the person to pressurise the most.

By choosing one person or group, change feels much more achievable. Be as specific as you can, as this holds your decision-maker accountable and makes it much more difficult for them to shift responsibility onto others and wriggle out of addressing the issue directly. It also means that tweets, letters, emails, and any other attempt to make noise about the issue can be directed at just one person, helping to make your mission more streamlined.

Tackling a taboo

One thought kept nagging at me. I knew from my own experience, from my friends, and from the media, that trying to effect *any* kind of change around a topic as stigmatised as periods wasn't going to be easy.

Shortly before, I'd read that a male MP in Westminster, while debating the tax we are forced to pay on (our 'luxury') period products, refused to say the word 'tampon'. He ducked and dived and could muster the courage only to say 'products'. Periods were just too embarrassing to be talked about in polite company, a dirty word, something shameful and revolting. I kept asking myself how on earth I was going to convince the Government to give free period products to schoolchildren, when some of the people who hold the power in Parliament couldn't even say the word 'period'!

I was guilty of it, too. Before starting Free Periods, I would whisper the word 'period' around other people and slip tampons up my sleeve when going to the bathroom at school. In public toilets, I ripped the sticky side of the pad off its plastic wrapper as slowly as I could, to avoid the embarrassment of that tell-tale sound. When I think back, that seems utterly ridiculous. Since I've started campaigning, I've gone into detail about my period on live TV and chanted about the mightiness of menstruation outside Parliament. But I never forget that I had also been socialised into believing that periods were something icky, something to hide, something disgusting, and definitely not something to talk about out loud.

It was only when I started thinking, really thinking, about why period poverty was such a huge problem across the globe, that I realised we were all complicit in putting up barriers which made it harder to normalise conversations about periods. We had all been part of the problem, part of the injustice.

There is a gendered stigma and shame imbued in the topic of menstruation. For too long, periods have been associated with dirt and disgust, with fear and impurity, and this needs to change. This entrenched culture of shame and secrecy is damaging, and we will never achieve true gender equality while periods are viewed as a source of embarrassment. I decided that through Free Periods, I would work to destigmatise the period, normalise menstruation conversation, and embrace language which is affirmative, empowering, and positive in its tone.

It takes courage to break through that discomfort. It takes strength to step forward and decide that *you* are the person to do something radically different. In thinking about who I was targeting, I realised that to be effective I had to do two things: not only convince the Government, but convince the public too.

No matter how taboo the topic may be, talking about it unapologetically will only have a positive impact. Sure, there will be people who give you sideways glances and snort in disgust, letting you know that they don't believe this to be a subject for everyday conversation, but it's important to jump from a place of safety and start getting comfortable with being uncomfortable. Society has conditioned us into thinking and behaving in certain ways, often subconsciously. We are taught from an early age to shy away from the topics that make us feel embarrassed or uneasy, and often these are the very issues that are blocking our way to equality or progress. They sit like giant rocks in our path and we need to pull together in big teams to hoist them up and move them to one side – and that happens only when one person decides that the time is now.

So, be the one who breaks through that blockade and shouts about the issues everyone is staying silent about. You can be the one to raise awareness of something hidden, or the one to speak up for the powerless or vulnerable who may not have the resources or confidence themselves to shout for change. When everyone else is too scared to talk about an issue, be the one to speak up. Question the stigma and interrogate it, and you will find that the door which was once closed will slowly begin to creak open.

Camryn Garrett was born and raised in New York. We met in Washington when we were on a panel together, and I was blown away by her confidence and eloquence. Camryn built an online following from a young age by speaking out on political and social issues, writing for big-hitting news outlets and at the age of 13 casually interviewing Warren Buffett for *Time* magazine.

An article about Angelina Jolie adopting a child who was thought to have AIDS roused Camryn's curiosity about the AIDS crisis; she started reading and researching, about both the disease itself and the activists fighting against the stigma. The more she read, the more she felt drawn to help destigmatise AIDS and raise awareness. Camryn decided to write a novel where the main protagonist was a teenage girl living a normal life with HIV. She tells me, 'I think there's a lot of public fear, which leads to people being unwilling to listen to issues concerning those affected by HIV. And that's definitely not an excuse for ignorance. I think people have this image in their minds of what HIV means, and it's usually someone getting really sick and dying, of pain, and of hurt.'

Camryn feels angry with the world, but I love that she harnessed her anger and used it to break a taboo in a brave and intimate way:

> I'm really angry about most things all of the time. There's so much injustice and so many horrible things happening on a small and large scale; there's war and there's racism and ignorance and wildfires and global warming. I think part of being a young person today is either being angry or fed up with the world we've been given. A lot of the time I feel hopeless, like there isn't anything I can do, but writing is something tangible that I *can* do. When it feels like no one is listening, I write, and a lot of the time, people are interested. Even if it's not a lot of people, there's usually one.

This has been her activism since she read that first article. When I ask her how she found the confidence and bravery to get started on something so bold, especially as a young person talking so frankly about an issue with so much stigma that didn't impact her directly, Camryn reminds me:

> Every single brave person you look up to has had this moment. They've all wondered what to do and how to start and have had moments of doubt. It's not about doing things perfectly on the first try or about being the best, but about doing it because you know how important it is. And once you start doing it, other people will let you know how much it means to them as well.

Hannah Witton is an award-winning YouTuber, broadcaster, and author. Her vlogs on sex, gender, body image, and feminism attract more than 24 million views on YouTube. She's certainly not one to shy away from talking about 'awkward' subjects. I ask her where she gets her confidence to dive into topics steeped in shame and stigma. Hannah tells me:

> To be honest, at the beginning I didn't find it that hard to speak openly about these taboo subjects, I just remember thinking, 'I'm comfortable speaking about sex and it's important, so I'm going to make YouTube videos about it!' I don't think, at the time, I realised the possible consequences of doing so, in terms of the number of people watching and the opportunities for harassment. If I started off knowing everything I know now, I think I would find it harder to open up. Maybe I should have been more scared of the internet at the beginning, but I'm glad I wasn't! One of the things that made it easier for me, I think, is that I really am deeply passionate about sex as a subject matter. I truly believe there is still a lot of work to do to rid ourselves of the shame surrounding sex and also how integral sex education is to wider topics such as health, economics, and equality.

Hannah tells me she doesn't find it surprising that it tends to be issues specific to women which are the most bound up in shame. She finds this both frustrating and infuriating. She posits that when men have had the loudest, or only, voices in the room for most of history, when 'women's issues' have been belittled and ignored, and women have been taught to not make a fuss, 'it's no wonder things like periods and clitoral pleasure feel like taboos'.

Her advice to someone who doesn't have the confidence to get started is that each of us has what it takes:

I always say: What's the one thing that makes you angry? What are you passionate about? Okay, can you start to talk about that with the people around you – friends, family? You're already making a difference! Are there any groups, in your local area (school/uni/workplace) or online that champion your cause that you can join and help out with? Do you have some spare time that you can use to volunteer with charities? We've all got what it takes to make a difference and change the world for the better, it's just about figuring out what you can do and working within your means, however limited your time or resources appear to be.

Adwoa Aboah tells me about the difficulty of overcoming trauma and pain through her activism, and the importance of destigmatising the taboo around mental health issues by creating a safe space at Gurls Talk for those who really need it. She tells me:

I feel sometimes I'm revisiting or reliving the trauma when I share my story, but at the same time, I hold so much respect for the dark days and I feel by not talking about them I'm not paying tribute to the journey I've been through to get where I am now. I personally find it grounds me and reminds me of how lucky I am to have made it through. I really don't want to glamorise the dark times, but it was a defining part of my life.

One of the most important aspects was freeing myself of shame. I didn't want to be afraid or suffocated by what had happened in the past. As a society, we attach so much shame to talking about mental health, and every time I or a member of the Gurls Talk community shares, I know we are helping fight that stigma. Nobody should be ashamed of struggling, and it's mine and Gurls Talks' duty to make sure we oppose that and actively create situations where gxrls can feel safe and supported enough to speak up.

I was privileged enough to have parents who could put me in treatment centres during my recovery, and, in these spaces, I encountered so many different kinds of people. Even though we were such a diverse group, what was apparent was that we had all experienced some of the same feelings and struggles. That completely diminished any sort of shame or stigma because we were all in the same boat and it was unlike anything I'd experienced before. I kept questioning why there hadn't been a space to delve into the problems that we dismissed when we were younger, but grew into bigger, important issues as we grew up. I had no education around anxiety or mental health and I had to examine what had gotten me to that place. I'm adamant that if I had been given a space like Gurls Talk maybe I wouldn't have gotten to such a sad place. People shouldn't have to hit rock bottom to receive help.

So, I ultimately started Gurls Talk because I wanted to create something preventative, a place that could replicate those intersectional spaces and help to educate and support young gxrls everywhere so they don't reach rock bottom. I wanted to soften the blow of going from an adolescent to an adult, to create a comfort blanket and space outside of school where gxrls could feel safe and be honest about all the things one goes through as a teenager. Retrospectively, I think I was searching for my own community in some ways too. After everything, I was finding out who I was, and seeking out people who would respect that growth and celebrate who I was becoming. That's how I feel in any Gurls Talk situation, it's truly like a family. That's how I want everyone in the community to feel so they can be their truest self.

As Adwoa's work to encourage honest and inclusive conversation around teenage mental health has shown, sharing your story and taking a stand can change the rules without you ever fully appreciating the impact you've had. For me, talking about periods openly became such a huge part of my campaigning. I knew the taboo and stigma surrounding menstruation were part of the problem and were preventing period poverty from being addressed. Children were not asking teachers, school nurses, or even their friends for help, because the shame and embarrassment was so entrenched that it was preferable to suffer in silence and alone. Even though I had been investing so much energy into lobbying the Government for free period products and swift action, I now discovered that by writing furiously about the need, by giving talks about why periods were holding children back, by talking nonstop about menstruation along with other activists, the subject of menstruation was being catapulted into the public consciousness like never before, and a menstrual movement was gaining steam across the globe. Remember that actions often ripple beyond their immediate place, platform, or moment.

When you decide to embark upon a journey to create change, no matter how trivial or minor you believe it to be, you could be creating something that grows beyond what you could ever see or imagine. In your campaigning and activism, in deciding to raise awareness of an issue that, up until now, has been hidden in the shadows, you could spark new conversations and change the dialogue. And the effects of what you do may not even be apparent to you. Some of the greatest victories are the ones we never get to see!

The solution

When I delved into the issue of period poverty, I could see that if we wanted to overcome the problem of pupils not going to school because they couldn't afford pads or tampons, these products would have to be provided for free.

Once you have your specific problem, you need a solution. I'm not saying this bit is always easy. I *know* it isn't. Even though you're confounded by a burning sense of injustice, it's not always straightforward to think of an immediate or logical solution that sounds reasonable.

A good place to start is to think of a world where this issue didn't exist. A perfect world. What does that world look like?

What will make the problem go away? What needs to change? The onus is on the campaigner to present a solution to the powers that be, to show them that change is achievable!

There are not many women like Edna Adan Ismail. She was Somaliland's first midwife, and set up her own hospital before becoming the First Lady and the country's first female cabinet minister. She is a formidable campaigner and pioneer for women's health. I was lucky enough to interview her in the summer of 2019, when she was in London promoting her book, and I was amazed at her ability to identify a problem, figure out a solution, and fearlessly make it happen. For her, finding solutions to the most entrenched of injustices was straightforward because her will to see change was powerful and unapologetic.

Edna was born in Somaliland, a country that remains culturally conservative, where women have limited agency, no voice and no power. When she was just eight, Edna's mother and grandmother arranged for a friend with no medical training to subject her to female genital mutilation (FGM), a brutal and primitive operation that involves cutting or removing some or all of the external female genitalia. In some countries, it's considered to be a form of 'purification', a belief grounded in gender inequality and a desire to limit women's sexuality. It can cause chronic pain, infections, increased risk of HIV transmission, birth complications, infertility, and even death.

Edna can still remember lying on the floor in shock, bleeding and crying in excruciating pain. It was a severely traumatic experience. Somaliland is a country with a population of 4 million, where 98 per cent of women between the ages of 15 and 49 have been subjected to FGM, and as an adult Edna realised that change was urgently needed. However, she knew that in a culturally sensitive climate, talking about FGM was dangerous.

Her solution was smart.

She talked about how FGM caused bleeding, infections, and possible infertility, rather than the trauma it caused. By approaching the topic from a health perspective, she didn't offend people but instead was able to sensitively and cleverly raise awareness of just how damaging FGM is to a girl. As a nurse, she had always spoken about the need for preventing diseases in children by vaccinating them, about attending prenatal check-ups and so on, and this was no different.

Sometimes your solution isn't as obvious as the problem itself. Think through different options and ask yourself whether the solution is specific enough to stop the problem you've identified. Is it something that can feasibly be done, or are you being too idealistic or too general? Period poverty is a global phenomenon ruining the lives of children everywhere. From Australia to Japan, across the length and breadth of Africa, from states in India and America to countries in Europe, students have told me that period poverty is hitting them hard. But there isn't a one-size-fits-all solution when each country has so many different cultural, social, and religious influences.

Look at recent developments in South Korea. I was recently contacted by a journalist from the capital, Seoul, who was writing a damning exposé about the pricing practices of some pad and tampon manufacturers in the region. We chatted for an hour over Skype about the news, which had taken Korean social media by storm.

When Yuhan-Kimberly, a leading manufacturer of pads in the region, announced a 20 per cent price hike on pads in May 2016, affecting 55 per cent of period products on the market, a torrent of stories poured forth. Suddenly this opened the floodgates for thousands to speak openly about their struggles to afford pads every month. News of the 'insole girls' dominated headlines – girls who admitted to wrapping toilet tissue around shoe insoles to create makeshift pads because they were already so unaffordable. The price increase would make pads between 50 per cent and 100 per cent more expensive than the same product sold in neighbouring countries, and people were rightly outraged.

In the gleaming, neon-lit city of Seoul, the stigma and taboo around periods was entrenched and menstruation was definitely a subject off-limits. Adverts for pads did not mention periods even once. In fact, periods are referred to as 'saengri' in Korea, which literally translates to 'physiological phenomenon', even though there is a word for menstruation, 'wolgyeong'. Even so, the activists infiltrated the public consciousness and have now begun to overthrow decades-old taboos around periods by carrying out different forms of activism, including performance art. South Korea has become an unlikely trailblazer in the use of menstrual cups and in offering menstrual leave, and the city provides free period products in a number of public places. It's incredible.

One thing to bear in mind is that you want to make it as

easy as possible for the person or people you're targeting to implement the change. You're much more likely to be successful if the solution is simple. In the early stages of Free Periods, I decided that the easiest solution would be for the state to give free products to those from low income families. My rationale was that the Government already had a list of the poorest children who were entitled to free school meals. They would be the ones who would need free products the most. But it soon became clear that it was more complicated to implement than I'd appreciated, and, as time went on, I started wondering how this would actually work in practice.

I could see a few pitfalls ahead, and people were routinely asking me how exactly the products would be distributed in a way that ensured those who needed them wouldn't be stigmatised or made to feel ashamed. It was a good point. The last thing I wanted was for students to be reluctant to claim their pads or tampons because it was embarrassing for them to present some sort of card at the local pharmacy. I realised that I needed to rethink my strategy.

I broadened the campaign to cover *all* children at school and not just those from the poorest families. That way, the Government could provide funding for products and the schools could leave them in bathrooms for anyone who needed them. It was also aligned with my fundamental belief that period products should be viewed in the same category as toilet paper or soap – a basic necessity. So, my solution to the problem of period poverty was now much broader. It might have been more costly for the Government to implement, but it would be easier to roll out.

It doesn't matter if you get it wrong at first. Nothing is ever set in stone, and it's absolutely OK for you to admit you've changed your mind. If you change tack and can explain why, that's even better! If not, you're probably the only person who will actually care. You'll gradually realise that your path to changemaking isn't linear. It might be diverted, and it will inevitably meander as your campaign progresses, but you have to stay positive – you're trying different approaches to get to your end goal. Any seasoned campaigner will tell you that they, too, have had to do this more times than they can remember!

See if you can find an example of where this solution has worked before. For me, Scotland was leading from the front in the fight against period poverty by offering free pads and tampons in schools and public places. This was actual, living proof that it could be done, and it was evidence of a progressive government choosing to prioritise the needs of those who menstruate. Throughout the campaign, I would refer to this over and over again. If they can do it, why can't we?

There were countries like Kenya, where two-thirds of women were unable to afford pads. In a country where the average daily wage is less than $2 a day, a study discovered that one in ten 15-year-old girls were selling sex to buy pads. In response, the Kenyan Government didn't just repeal tax on pads and tampons to lower the price; it also allocated funding for free pads to be distributed in schools.

Similarly, in Kerala, in Southern India, all schools are given free pads, storage, and eco-friendly incinerators. These became my examples time and again, and as I found more countries making similar pledges, I added them to the list. If they were doing it, we needed to follow suit!

In 2015, Josie Naughton was the PA to Coldplay's manager, having spent ten years working her way up the ranks in the music industry. That year, the refugee crisis exploded. A million people, looking for sanctuary after fleeing war and persecution, arrived in Europe. Families from countries including Syria, Afghanistan, Iraq, Eritrea, and South Sudan were walking staggering distances to cross borders, living in makeshift camps, and getting into dinghies and risking their lives. They simply had no other choice.

Within a few months, Josie had co-founded Help Refugees, now one of the most successful humanitarian response charities in Europe, working with 125 grassroots organizations in 14 countries and supporting over 100,000 refugees. Their charity has had the backing of big celebrity names such as Emma Thompson, Alexa Chung, Louis Theroux, and Judi Dench, and they've even collaborated with the street-artist Banksy. Josie tells me:

Despite displacement being an issue for decades, it was only in 2015 that the term 'refugee crisis' really entered our vocabulary. I was putting links on Facebook to articles and petitions that sometimes I hadn't even read or signed myself. Then the realisation hit, that sometimes if you want things to change you have to roll up your sleeves and do it yourself. Together with friends Dawn O'Porter and Lliana Bird, we decided to raise £1,000 and get hold of one van-load of tents and sleeping bags to take to Calais in Northern France. The links we set up went viral and within a week we had raised £56,000 and were receiving 7,000 packages of aid (primarily from our Amazon Wish List) every single day. We needed volunteers to assist with putting everything into our storage space in North London which we had managed to get for free and so, again, we turned to social media to ask for help. People showed up from all walks of life and before we knew it, we had almost 20 rooms of sorted aid – enough for several artic lorries.

We suddenly realised that we didn't know who any of this aid or funding was going to and felt a real sense of responsibility from the public who had trusted us to get everything to where it was most needed. I, along with three others who had volunteered (Philli and Dani, who are both still part of the core team), set off to Calais, expecting to find a large traditional aid organisation or governmental body taking care of everyone.

Instead, Josie found 5,000 people living in a field:

Many of them had no food, shelter, or even shoes. There was little access to water. We met children as young as nine living completely on their own in the same conditions. (I later learnt that the correct term was 'unaccompanied minors'.) Winter was coming and people needed shelter; human beings living like this anywhere in the world, let alone in Europe, was unacceptable. We couldn't unsee what we had witnessed, so we partnered with a local French association called L'auberge de migrants, rented a warehouse, and began a shelter-building programme. Using social media, we asked for volunteers and established ourselves as an umbrella to a number of grassroots organisations working to meet the needs of a refugee camp that 10,000 people had now come to inhabit.

At the same time, in Greece, up to 10,000 people were arriving in a single day. Once again, it was everyday people who were stepping up and saving lives. Josie and the team flew in doctors, supported local people to cook thousands of meals, found fishermen to do search and rescue, supported mass distributions of aid, and filled the gaps left by governments and NGOs.

'This is where the model of what we do now began,' Josie tells me. Fast forward five years, Help Refugees works cross-sector, doing everything from supporting children's hospitals, conducting search and rescue organisations, to education and creating safe spaces for women. They have been powered by over 30,000 volunteers and raised over £30,000,000. 'We are driven by needs, and as long as people are being denied their most basic human rights we will strive to choose love and change that.'

I was particularly interested in how creatively Josie came up with a solution to raise money and awareness of the refugee crisis. The charity desperately needed an injection of funds to help thousands survive the bitter winter of 2017. They needed a new, fresh fundraising idea. The Choose Love shop was the answer, and the premise was beautifully simple.

Now with branches in in New York, Los Angeles, and London, these are shops where you can buy everyday items like a child's coat, a sleeping bag, or a tent for a refugee rather than yourself. You can also buy items that represent services – a school bag serves as education, for example. The shops also work to educate the consumer. Choose Love shows those of us privileged enough to live in developed communities that people deserve to have more than just their basic needs met. Emotional and mental health support (represented by a tissue box) is equally important.

We wanted the store to feel current and cool, again moving away from the traditional charity shop, so it was designed with a nod to our favourite retail space, the Apple store. Very simple, with a huge 'Choose Love' sign, of course. We have a long table down the middle (like the Apple store tables) where you can look at the items, touch them, and connect to the people on the other end. It's a very emotional experience for a lot of people, realising there are children without shoes, women and girls without access to sanitary items, and that they can make a simple purchase to change that.

My friends and I visited the London store, just off Carnaby Street, in December 2018. For Christmas that year, I gave my parents and brother a card each (with beautiful portrait images on the front taken on the ground at refugee camps) from the Choose Love store; instead of a present for them that year, I'd bought gifts for refugees on their behalf.

When the London store opened, its motto was to 'Shop your heart out, leave with nothing, and feel the love'. The concept has raised over £3 million to date. 'People love transparency, the directness and knowing exactly what their money will be spent on,' says Josie.

> I never imagined that I would be the CEO of an organisation working in three continents and if I had set out to do that, I probably wouldn't have got here. I often come back to the saying 'Don't let perfection be the enemy of good.' Don't worry about failing or making mistakes. Just do everything one step at a time. Taking that first step can feel scary but just remember, you have to start somewhere. If you don't try, then you won't ever make that difference. I truly believe anything is possible if you put your mind to it.

Listen

It's always a good idea to 'test out' your idea, so talk to those closest to you first. Think of it like an activist focus group, where you sound out your thoughts and explain why this is the issue that has spurred you into action. Explain your core message, who you're targeting for a solution and why, and share ideas of how you're going to get to your goal. Be honest and open to the response you get – don't just hear the good things. The feedback may reflect the thoughts of others, which, once your campaigning is out there in the world, will be amplified and multiplied!

When I found out that children were missing school because they couldn't afford period products, I told my friends at school, who were equally incensed. The one question I was asked over and again was, 'Are you sure it's happening in the UK? It can't be.' My friends had heard about period poverty happening in other countries, but there was so little awareness of it happening right under our noses. There was a sense of collective outrage.

I could see that my school friends and family would be most likely to agree with me, so I decided to canvas feedback from people who might take a different view, or who might not have thought very much about the issue at all, to gather more of a range of perspectives.

This bit was difficult, and I was completely out of my comfort zone. I asked boys I knew, and some of my brother's friends, to gauge their opinion. Don't be disillusioned if people think you're totally crazy. I knew straight away that talking about periods was not going to be easy, and I've lost count of the number of times people have changed the subject from periods to just about anything else mid-conversation! But I knew that having those conversations was crucial if I wanted to find out what people thought about the issue I was going to tackle.

Many of those boys I asked were so uncomfortable that the conversations were more or less non-starters. I was met with awkward grunts and red faces. My brother cringed at my audacity, but some of his friends actually offered some really valuable thoughts, mainly about how to bring cis boys into the conversation when they didn't feel as though it was theirs to have. Many of them remembered being separated from the girls in their class to be taught sex education, or being left in bewilderment when the 'time of the month' or 'PMS' was mentioned in conversation. One told me, 'The thing is with periods, you don't even know what you don't know.' We discussed the importance of educating the next generation of cis boys about periods, in order to normalise them in society.

When I mentioned the campaign to some people, they asked me: Why periods? If I wanted to fight for something, why periods? Of all things, periods? Period poverty in the UK affected only a very small number of children, so why not do something bigger? Porn culture, racial discrimination, and air pollution were all suggested as issues that were a better use of my time. But there was no way I was going to let these comments shake my conviction, and neither should you, because there will always be people who won't take you seriously, who will trivialise and belittle what you're trying to do. Who cares?

Sophie Walker has (rightly) been referred to as a 'modern-day suffragette'. After leaving her job as an international reporter and editor at Reuters, Sophie became the leader of the Women's Equality Party, standing for London Mayor in 2016 and campaigning relentlessly for gender equality, women's rights and representation, and disability rights. She's now Chief Executive of Young Women's Trust, a UK charity campaigning for economic justice for women aged 18–30. Every time I've met Sophie, her compassion, indestructible energy, and sheer passion has reinforced my faith in the future of feminism.

When I ask her about how she stays resilient when faced with those questioning the need for feminist activism and minimising her work, she tells me:

I have learnt not to give my precious energy away to those who debate in bad faith. I used to think I owed it to the sisterhood to take on those who would argue against feminism and women's equality – but I have learnt over the years to be more discriminating about those encounters. I'm not interested in any more public debates on whether we need feminism – I'm not interested in giving a platform to misogynists in nice suits. I block and mute a lot on social media. The devil has enough advocates.

That said, I do want to discuss with people who want to understand more and come with an open mind. It's very important to me that as activists we create and curate safe spaces – that is, spaces in which to safely encounter and discuss different ideas with mutual respect. I worry about 'cancel culture' and simply shutting down those who disagree. I understand how hard that is. As activists, we come to the fight often with our own painful experiences and vulnerabilities. Sharing our thoughts for others' consideration is hard. It's very common to view criticism or an alternative view as a negation of your experience. But we need to get past that. The only successful campaign is one that wins a considered argument. Not one that shuts other people down.

It's really important to approach alternative opinions with nuance and composure. If people doubt you, your bank of evidence will arm you with an incontestable argument for why change is needed. Before you start your campaign, try to gauge how different people might poke holes in what you're fighting for, and think about how you're going to respond and educate them. Speak to people older than you, younger than you, who have no understanding of what you're addressing, and you'll be ready for anything.

Channel your anger

When I read about period poverty that cold day in April, I was angry. Whenever I had some spare time at school, I would search the internet for related articles on the subject. And when I went back to whatever I was doing, I'd still feel the anger and sadness burn in me. It started dominating my thoughts. I kept thinking about those students missing school because they were poor. Month after month, year after year. No help was coming to them, no adult in a position of power was moved enough to act.

Rage can be one of the most productive and useful tools to have in your arsenal. Taking that anger and turning it into something powerful can be liberating and galvanising.

I'd never been angrier than when I read some of the 517 comments made in response to an article published in the second most widely read English news site in the world (yes, that one). It was about me and the campaign, and it was published in October 2017, just a week after I'd turned eighteen. I could feel that the issue of period poverty was finally starting to make a dent in the public consciousness. I'd been interviewed by an earnest journalist, and the article was out a few days later, on a Saturday morning. One of my teachers emailed me excitedly to say he'd just seen the article, and as I pulled it up on my phone, all I could see was comment after comment popping up under the article. The comments were scathing. Most had a tone of mocking or derision, and the more I read, the angrier I became. Here is a flavour:

'Stop wanting handouts all the time. What are you raising awareness for? Women have had periods since the beginning of time love.'

'No more dinner time adverts about these products. Keep it to "that" aisle in Boots.'

'Soon they'll be looking for free undies.'

'How about making your own from torn up sheets? How about some personal responsibility?'

'They should go out and buy less trendy clothes. And stop going out drinking and having your hair coloured and nose rings and tattoos.'

'Can I have free razors? And plasma TVs.'

And my personal favourite… 'We need to wipe our behind don't we? Same thing.'

The comments kept spooling out. The ones which were personal, about my appearance or skin colour, got deleted very quickly, but not before I could read them. Some of the comments were trolling and vicious. I could feel myself physically folding inwards, my face burning, ashamed that people I knew would be reading them, too. I felt panicked, a rush of pain, hot tears burning the back of my eyes.

It would have been easy for me to let those words tear me into pieces. Instead, I could feel the rage burn as I absorbed the lack of empathy and sarcasm directed towards those struggling to cope with their period every month. It hit a nerve. I was seething at the level of ignorance and cruelty. I had to do something. I sat down behind my desk and furiously wrote a blog post on how period poverty was hitting teenagers hard, and why it was time for people to stop ignoring or belittling the issue.

As a girl, I was told that being angry is bad. When we're angry or upset, we are often dismissed as strident, shrill, and overbearing. Boys, on the other hand, are encouraged from a young age to be forthright, to stand up for themselves, or retaliate bravely, to shout out and take control. Their anger defines them as confident, capable, and assertive. They don't put up with any nonsense and they're often reminded that these characteristics mark them out as leaders. As we grow older, girls suppress their anger, downplaying their personal power and agency to avoid an uncomfortable situation. How can we not when after expressing our strong feelings we are told to 'calm down, dear' (David Cameron) or are slammed as being 'nasty women' (Donald Trump), or for expressing 'female rage'? In a Grand Slam final in September 2018, Serena Williams was punished by a male umpire for breaking her racket by throwing it to the ground, in response to the accusation that she cheated. Many soon pointed out that the public and press's response to her anger was sexist and racialised, and would probably not have been as extreme if she were a man. The outcry over Williams' anger was certainly symptomatic of society's expectation that women must always be graceful and calm, even in the face of unfairness.

In the words of the incredible Chimamanda Ngozi Adichie: 'We teach girls to shrink themselves, to make themselves smaller. We say to girls, you can have ambition but not too much. You should aim to be successful, but not too successful. Otherwise, you will threaten the man.'

It's what we've been conditioned to do. So, we suppress our instinct to speak up and shout out.

I asked my amazing friend, the comedian and activist Grace Campbell, about how she's used anger productively. She tells me:

I think you have to be angry as an activist, anger is what fuels the fire in you and pushes you to keep fighting for the change you want to make. The thing about activism is you have to really care so much about something because you're going to have to patiently fight – this stuff doesn't happen overnight. I think anger does fuel that kind of effort. The key is to know when to display the anger, because there are certain situations where you need to use more diplomatic energies to get your point across, in a kill-the-haters-with-kindness kind of way. But I think generally anger is good; if you're angry, you will make change, big or small, there's no doubt about that.

I hate when my anger, or a woman's anger, is weaponised against us to make us look weak, or hysterical. Especially because there are such extreme double standards here. When a man displays his anger it's just a man displaying his anger, and no one uses that against him to try to make him look weak. I think you have to be aware of this and prepare for the fact that when you have anger, there will be people who will use it against you. But also, do you care what those people think if those are the exact people who would accept that kind of behaviour in a man? You can't get caught up stressing about what those people think because they already want you to fail.

My great-grandma died a couple of years ago, at the age of 89. She's my ultimate feminist heroine. The course of her life had been prescribed from a young age. Growing up in India in the 1930s, she understood that society's expectation of her was to be a housewife and mother, but not much more. It was just the 'natural order of things'.

Her two brothers went to school and were encouraged to excel. They went on to university and were expected to flourish academically. My great-grandma had to fight to be allowed to go to university. She was bright and curious. Throughout her teens and into her twenties, she felt a growing sense of unease, a low grumble of anger that she put a lid on. As her brothers went on to become accomplished in academia and business, she married and started a family. But she wanted more.

Her sense of rebelliousness and burning ambition struck me even as a child. Sitting in the verandah at the front of her house on a balmy evening during a family holiday to India, I interrogated her about her life, in awe at her determination and refusal to live according to traditional expectations. 'I just needed more,' she told me. 'Women could do so much, but we were in shackles.' In her thirties, she did something very few women did at the time. She applied to do a Masters in America. Leaving her husband and children behind, she left to study journalism. She had never left India and never even seen a plane, let alone flown in one. Hers was a story of courage and self-belief, of liberating her rage for good.

She graduated and returned to her family after two years, eventually becoming a leading journalist and lecturer, specialising in women's health. When I think about that mute anger she'd contained inside for years, the internal tussle between conforming and rebelling, I wonder how she did it. I wonder how different her life would have been if she hadn't listened to the constant rumble of rage; if she'd decided not to turn that anger into something else?

When we see barriers, hypocrisies, and misrepresentations, I believe we can turn that anger into a powerful force for change, for ourselves and for everything and everyone around us. Don't ignore it. Don't keep telling yourself it will go away. Acknowledge it's there and use it as a springboard to start fighting and keep going.

There were days during my campaigning where I would feel as though everything was too still and uneventful. Sometimes, in between school, family, and seeing friends, I would feel helpless. I didn't know what my next step should be, and how I could up the ante of Free Periods. It was coasting. I was coasting. During those times, I would sometimes reread my emails from girls who had contacted me before. The girl who told me how she'd been laughed at in school that day because she'd bled onto her uniform, the girl whose mum hadn't been at home for two days when she needed money to buy pads, the girl who had to stay at home because she couldn't bring herself to ask a parent for money when she knew there wasn't any. I would reread emails from the MPs who would politely tell me that they wouldn't be taking action because schools had funding which they could use however they wanted, or from trolls who would tell me that I was a stupid, dumb teenager who wanted something for nothing.

Something would be reignited in me when I connected with that anger. It would feel like a rush of air behind me pushing me forward.

Gina Martin is a perfect example of someone who used her anger to make a real difference. At a music festival in Hyde Park in the summer of 2017, she spotted a photo on a man's phone of a woman's underwear and thighs. She was shocked to realise that it was her body; she'd been 'upskirted', photographed without her knowledge or consent. She reported it to the police, but there was nothing they could do, as it was not legally classed as a sexual offence.

She soon launched the campaign #StopSkirtingTheIssue, along with a petition that raised over 111,000 signatures. After two years of working with lawyer Ryan Whelan to persuade politicians to take the issue seriously, she had changed the law in England and Wales, and upskirting was made illegal; those convicted now face up to two years in prison.

I asked Gina what spurred her to take a stand, and how she stayed so driven, even when it felt like her campaigning wasn't going anywhere.

I honestly think initially it was just the straw that broke the camel's back. I was so tired of brushing off stuff like that and I'd done everything asked of me; get the evidence, get witnesses, defend yourself, make people aware – so when I found out it wasn't a sexual offence and they dropped my case I just got unbelievably angry. I guess, beforehand, I'd internalised and maybe somewhat believed that the other things that happened to me hadn't been dealt with because *I* hadn't reacted well enough. After the upskirting incident I rejected that idea and decided to stand up and get angry because I'd done *everything* 'right' and had discovered this gaping hole in the law. I felt it would have been inhuman to ignore that, and I was bored of people in power ignoring it for us.

I relied really heavily on the people around me to pick me up when I was losing hope, which I think is something we often don't talk about in campaigner/activism spaces. The new-feminist narrative of a woman staying strong, independent, and bossing it is far more sellable, but in reality, I leant really hard on those around me. I also often think that the reason I kept going when the campaign wasn't doing anything in the early days is because I'd picked the right fight. I chose to fight against something that had affected me. That was part of me.

Rage is good, and it's powerful. When we realise that we can use our anger as a transformative force, we start to resist in a different way. We resist with more hunger and single-mindedness and the anger burns as fuel.

CHAPTER 2

FIND YOUR CROWD

Making allies

No matter how determined or seasoned an activist you are, you can't do this alone.

Activism is about rallying people behind a cause. The more people there are with you and the greater the force behind you pushing you forward, the more likely you are to make change.

You are only one part of a much bigger picture. One thing I've found during campaigning is that there really is incredible, lightning energy generated when we start to see each other and listen to each other. There is so much power in working together, and feeling part of something much bigger than yourself. Your own story is going to be incredible, but it's just the beginning. To get to where you want to be, you need other people to lift you up and help you thrive, to carry you when you lose momentum or flounder. And in doing the same back, you're helping to build up a community and network of people who are ready to charge forward and make amazing things happen.

I've been honoured to have been invited to Bill and Melinda Gates' Goalkeepers event in New York a couple of times. Every time I've gone, I have been totally blown away by just how many people have dedicated themselves to make our world better, often while holding down another job, sometimes two or even three, and dealing with all sorts of unique challenges. During the event, it's so joyful to see numbers being exchanged, email addresses and cards passed from hand to hand with the words: 'Let's keep in touch.' The air in the auditorium dances with hope and optimism. It reminds us how lucky we are to be part of something exciting, something bigger than just ourselves. It reminds us how lucky we are to live in a world where people take up the work of activism, of fighting for the good of others, and dedicate their lives to it.

It's where I met Buddhist monk Wangchuk Rapten, a paramedic and outreach worker from Nepal. Dressed in his red robes, he held my gaze with his gentle smile. Rapten lost his mother to jaundice when he was 13. They didn't have the money to take her to Kathmandu for the treatment that most likely would have cured her. He now offers healthcare at his Nepalese clinic for just Rs5 (equivalent to about 5 pence), so that no one is deprived of medical attention.

Goalkeepers is also where I met Trisha Shetty, an Indian activist for gender equality and founder of SheSays, a platform to educate, rehabilitate, and empower women to take direct action against sexual assault in India. It's where I realised just how critical it is to join forces, to build up a wall of supportive arms; arms that will be there for you even on the most rubbish days when you feel you don't know what you're doing and where on earth you're going.

Think of all the hard-hitting movements that have pushed through incredible change. Think about Greta Thunberg, who cut a lonely and isolated figure as she sat in her yellow raincoat in front of the Swedish parliament when she started her one-person school strike for climate action. That figure is anything but solitary now. Just look at the millions of people who demonstrated in marches across different time zones and countries to demand urgent action to tackle the climate crisis. Look at the explosion of the vast and growing youth movement she has brought about, and just look at how world leaders stand motionless when she cries out through tears, 'How dare you?'

As young people, as women, people of colour or from a minority community, it's so easy to resign ourselves to the feeling that, alone, we can't do very much. In fact, even without all these elements stacked against us, society teaches us to be individualistic, competitive, selfish, and self-reliant. We are told to pit ourselves against each other, to be singular.

I could never have made it this far by myself. Without every signature on the Free Periods petition, without every shouting voice and colourful banner at our protest, without every penny donated to our legal challenge, the campaign would never have morphed into what it eventually became.

By campaigning together, by dividing and conquering, by plotting and planning with people just like you, a collective voice will boom. Finding your crowd is like snuggling under a warm blanket, or being squished in the fold of a hug that tells you you're not battling alone. Campaigning can be lonely work sometimes, and I remember all too clearly feeling as if all I was doing was bellowing into a vacuum and that any minute now, I'd lose my voice completely.

I realised this too late in the day, but trying to do everything on your own isn't going to get you far. There were days I felt as though I was wading through thick mud, in stilettos, in the rain. I felt panicked and overwhelmed. We'll consider this later (see Chapter 5), but looking after your mental health is essential. How will you make the world better if you're not taking care of yourself? Not reaching out for help when you need it will leave you feeling burnt out and depleted. We can't escape from it – the reality is that the ebbs and flows of campaigning are often punctuated with moments when you feel that too much has to be done to achieve something small. I remember it well: to get the go-ahead for one op-ed (opinion pieces, which in print newspapers are usually opposite the page that expresses the paper's editorial view) in one publication meant spending hours writing pitches to many. Then one tweet from someone with a massive social media following would come out of nowhere after I'd contacted fifty celebrities and been ignored. And sometimes, it would take over twenty emails to different MPs to get just one reply.

It can be utterly exhausting to invest so much of yourself into something, and not really know if anything worthwhile will come out of it. I must have burnt millions of calories from stress! I wanted to do everything perfectly, and at a furious pace. I soon found out that my campaign was too big to take on alone, and my mental health depended on sharing the load.

Start by finding your people. Look online or ask around to find people working towards a similar outcome. Note down all the other activists and organisations you find. You need to research their mission, their call-to-arms, their strategy and successes. Then, reach out to them and tell them what you plan to achieve. Ask about working together. You will be bolstered by their tactics, their spirit and defiance. I did this, contacting other people who were also working towards ending period poverty in some way, and there it was. The same stories, the same anger, the familiar frustrations, the much-needed 'I know exactly how you feel' reassurances. They were behind me, and we had each other's backs. We anchored ourselves to each other and we shared opportunities with each other.

I got in touch with Tina Leslie, the founder of Freedom4Girls, the brilliant charity that sends pads to schoolchildren in Kenya, to see if we could work together. A few days later, she told me that she was going to talk about period poverty on a BBC radio show and asked if I would consider appearing alongside her. Of course I would, I told her.

It was a weekday, and I wasn't able to leave school to go to the studios. Instead, at breaktime, I found an empty class to dial into the call with the producer who was preparing me for my role as a guest alongside Tina. She warned me that if the programme overran, there was a strong possibility that my bit might get cut out. I remember waiting with clammy palms for the call to say that it was my slot, but when my phone rang, it was an apologetic call to let me know that they were running behind schedule, so there was only time to take listener's calls. I was so disappointed!

As I walked back to class, feeling really disheartened, Tina texted me with an idea. She suggested I dial into the phone-in as one of the listeners. That way, I would still get to talk about Free Periods and ask people to sign the petition. I rushed out of the classroom, back into the corridor and called into the show. I got through. I had only two minutes – where the presenter was clearly playing devil's advocate, challenging what I was saying and interjecting with questions – but it worked. Thousands of people had now heard the words Free Periods, and I could see an immediate spike in the number of signatures on the petition. I felt pretty pleased as I went back to my lesson. When I walked in, the entire class cheered. I had no idea that they had all been listening. It dawned on me that what I needed was people. The feeling that my friends in class had my back, and Tina was there to help boost my campaign was exactly what I needed.

Sometimes these opportunities might come along when you least expect them, and turn into something you would have never predicted. With Free Periods, this has happened more times than I can count! Here are a few examples.

Many months after the campaign's creation, I teamed up with a feminist collective called The Pink Protest, founded by Scarlett Curtis, Grace Campbell, Honey Ross, and Alice Skinner. Meeting them was a fluke, which came off the back of a holiday cancelled at the eleventh hour, meaning I had a free week with no plans. A random request dropped into my inbox at the beginning of the week, through a sister of a friend, to take part in an interview series the Pink Protest were shooting about what it means to be an activist. It was going to feature Jameela Jamil, Emma Freud, and others. I was excited.

The next day, I met Scarlett and Grace in West London, and we hit it off instantly. As soon as the interview was filmed, we huddled together in Scarlett's kitchen and started hatching plans, plotting ideas of how we could work together and make some proper noise. They were looking to support activists working on their own campaigns, to help amplify their message by joining forces. Scarlett returned to New York for the next semester of her degree, so any protest planning relied firmly on after-school Skype calls, interspersed with endless emails and WhatsApp messages exchanged in the early hours of the morning. Alice, a talented illustrator, created some powerful images which we used throughout the campaign, my favourite being a woman lying in a bath filled with tampons with the caption: This is What Luxury Looks Like. A not-so-subtle dig at how period products are classed as luxury products, instead of basic essentials.

I still say that organising a protest must be a bit like planning a wedding, except you have no clue how many people will actually turn up. And there are no presents. And no flowers. And no embarrassing uncle. But we had to get a stage, arrange speeches, food, drink, and music. And keep praying that a few people – not just our closest friends – would make an appearance. To this day, I break out in a little sweat when I think of how much we had to do to navigate the logistics, but without Scarlett and Grace, it wouldn't have happened. Meeting them and knowing that they wanted the Free Periods protest to be a roaring success was a game-changer for me. I didn't realise how much I needed that feeling of togetherness when I'd been campaigning on my own for over seven months, and meeting them marked a new energy in my own efforts.

Soon after the protest, I received an email from Janvi Patel, a British lawyer based in Los Angeles. We arranged a call, and Janvi spoke excitedly about the idea of launching a legal challenge against the British Government, to urge them to take action to end period poverty in schools. Her premise was that, under the Equality Act 2010, the Government has a legal obligation to make sure that all children have equal access to education. If periods are a barrier to children receiving that education, the Government must put in place measures to ensure that barrier no longer exists. So, providing free pads or tampons in schools would allow those who were missing school because of period poverty to start attending lessons. It was exciting to think that we had a different route to explore, something that had the potential to force the Government's hand into finally taking decisive action. Drawing upon Janvi's experience, we decided we would look into a legal challenge, and within weeks, we were meeting with human rights lawyers at Hausfeld, and renowned barristers at their chambers to see how we could make it happen.

About one month later, at a launch event for a nail polish (random!), I met Gemma Abbott. Gemma was also a lawyer, running the Hackney branch of the Red Box Project, a charity that distributes pads and tampons in red boxes to schools for whoever needs them. We'd followed each other on social media for ages, and I was in awe at all the work the Red Box Project was doing. In the usual pattern of things, we started ranting about the Government's inaction against period poverty, and wondering whether they would ever commit to ending it through provision of period products in schools. Six months later, as part of the groundwork for the legal challenge, Free Periods had become a company limited by guarantee and, Janvi, Gemma, as well as the cofounders of the Red Box Project, Clegg Bamber and Anna Miles, were on the Board of Directors. Soon, we were holding weekly meetings and phone calls with lawyers and discussing our fundraising strategy in the run-up to launching our very own legal case. Janvi, Gemma, and Clegg are still Directors of Free Periods Limited, and together we're continuing to fight for menstrual equity and raise awareness of the Government scheme that provides period products in schools. Who would have thought it?

I asked Minna Gillett, a friend from school and supremely talented artist, to create images for us to share on social media, which we then used for publicity for the legal campaign. Minna's illustrations were striking, bold, and unique. She was already a huge supporter of the campaign and was so happy to get involved – it was the perfect collaboration.

A few months later, I was approached online by Olivia Kiernan, a London-based Insight Executive with experience in digital campaigning and data and behavioural economics. She was passionate about our mission to end period poverty and keen to help in any way, with an expertise that hinged on marketing and research. Before long, she and I met at her office, and she presented some fantastic research on period poverty, which was crucial to building our long-term strategy.

My point is this: you never know when something truly

amazing is around the corner. Keep an eye out for people who can help you. It doesn't matter how big or small your campaign is, pull together as much talent as possible. Contact other passionate activists, campaigners, and organisations, set up a phone call or meet for coffee, and think of ways you can use your separate campaigns and supporters to build something bigger, together.

Gabby Edlin, founder of the charity Bloody Good Period, which provides period products to those who can't afford them, agrees. Even though our work is slightly different, our mutual passion for menstrual equity and an end to period poverty in the UK has meant we've been able to collaborate on different projects and campaigns over the last few years. Gabby says:

Collaboration is everything! It's not only power in numbers, but it's where you learn from each other too.

Collaborating with other organisations is so crucial, because our causes are not only intersectional, but they overlap too, and this is where you can hold a united voice. For example, Free Periods and BGP can happily shout for one another because some school children are refugees and some refugees are school children, and we both believe in free provision of products.

I think there's sometimes a misunderstanding that collaborating means merging – early on in BGP, quite a few people (cis men) advised I merge BGP under a bigger charity, but I knew if I did, then the power would be lost. Instead, as a smaller organisation, we find we have more power working on projects or campaigns alongside other small to medium groups – it means our individual voices aren't lost under corporate speak, and things aren't slowed down by bureaucracy!

She believes that inclusivity and diversity in activism is vital, even in the world of period-related activism:

> It's not just important to show different skin tones (although representation is vital), it's about diversity of thought. This is particularly important in the period space, as our various cultures, countries we come from, where our parents come from, our traditions, religions, and upbringings will impact the way we feel about menstruation. Having points of view that diverge from the 'standard' white cis woman is absolutely crucial in creating a variety of solutions for period poverty.

Don't be afraid to ask your immediate circles – your friends, family, colleagues – for help or advice. Even if it's just proof-reading an email, or doing something simple and admin-y. It's not a sign of weakness to ask for help, especially in the early stages of the campaign when it can feel utterly overwhelming. It's freeing. It gives your thinking new perspective. I asked my local councillor if he could help, and I put posters up in my local library and in the toilets at school, asking for volunteers.

Accept any help you're offered. Write down what your campaign needs today, next month, and in the next six months, and see if you can match up those offers and skills to exactly what you need. Bear in mind that terrible, clichéd phrase: 'Teamwork makes the dream work.' It's true.

If I listed all the individuals, friends, family, charities, and organisations that helped me along the way, it would fill up this entire book, but most of those offers of help came from being bold enough to ask – even though a lot of the time, I wasn't really sure what I was asking for.

Raise an internet army

Your online friends are *so* important. Our collective power can achieve so much more than one voice alone, so it's really vital that you grow your online community and keep them engaged and enthusiastic about your cause.

Without realising it's happening, you'll accumulate a community of people, activists, and organisations that will add depth, strength, and vision to your mission.

The thing is, a campaign is not just about you. It belongs to everyone. You have to be prepared to offer your newly hatched campaign to everyone. You want them all to own a bit of it, because that's when you start to capitalise on skills, talents, and everything that other people have to offer. That's when you feel a force surrounding you, urging you on, because everyone around you is pushing for change, not just you.

Invite people to share artwork and images that you can post on Twitter and Instagram. Ask people to write blogs and share poems or articles. Encourage people to offer up ideas and suggestions about what they want to see and what you can do better. In starting Free Periods, I knew I was privileged to be able to drive forward something quite special, and it felt like we were on the cusp of exciting change. But I also knew I was just a teenager who needed help and direction, and being honest and upfront about that drew in other people. I noticed that more and more people had started to add #FreePeriods, or the petition link, to their Instagram and Twitter bios. Clearly, Free Periods meant something to a lot of people. It was a movement that they were part of, it was theirs too, and they wanted it to be a success as much as I did.

Building an online community and knowing that this is a shared fight suddenly makes change feel more achievable. Send out regular updates via email or social media so people always feel connected and involved. Be open and sincere. At the core of all your communication should be the reasons why this matters so much to you – so, more than anything, be authentic.

Try to be confident in your tone, too, because it implies a modicum of ambition and determination, which is contagious. You want people to know they're part of something big.

Keep the wording in all your online communication really positive. There's a paradox there. How can an issue that's plainly ignored by those who have the power to reverse it, an issue that incites red hot fury inside you, *not* have you angry and frothing? And how can it be right *not* to convey that rage to those who support the same cause? It can feel counterintuitive, but what I've found is that keeping a sense of perspective and focusing on the positive actions we can all undertake, rather than being overtly combative or angry, seems to get more responses, with more people wanting to get involved. I learnt quickly that a dash of anger was good, but it was always more effective to counterbalance that with a more empowered, controlled tone.

If you decide to start a petition, remember to spend some time every week scrolling down the list of comments. I used to do this every day at the outset. For me, it was a curious tonic. I found it incredibly reassuring to read encouragement from people I had never met.

It soon became apparent that many of the people who had added their names to the petition had been through period poverty themselves, and some would describe their own experiences. I would find myself feeling both sad and hopeful, in equal measure. Those comments were wonderfully galvanising and acted as constant reminders throughout the campaign that this wasn't going to be an easy fight. It was clear that very little had changed for decades, but I sure as hell wasn't going to be the one to give up.

I came across one comment from a Board member of ActionAid who had signed the petition and asked if she could help. Margaret Casely-Hayford left an email address, signalling her genuine intent. When I wrote back, her response was kind and uplifting, full of subtle praise and words of advice. She copied me into letters she'd written to different organisations where she had contacts, to celebrities, and to publications, asking them to help me. Finding allies like Margaret boosted me and it felt like people out there had my back.

Allies are essential and incredibly valuable. Together, you can weather the responses of the naysayers and shrug off the inflammatory comments. You simply can't campaign successfully without your community, so do everything you can to make sure they feel important, involved, and invested in the movement. Each online follower is an essential activist, and they must know that they are part of something big, meaningful, and worth fighting for.

The bigger picture

As mentioned earlier, when you're collaborating, see if your campaign taps into something bigger. I thought about period poverty as sitting in the middle of a Venn diagram, because struggling to afford period products has health, social, and financial implications. These were big, umbrella issues that drove inequality and hampered progress towards a better world, and period poverty sat in the space where they overlapped.

It's a good idea to think about the wider issues to which your activism relates. You can even draw your own Venn diagram. If you're tackling homelessness, then poverty and health are both the cause and the effect. If it's climate change, then global health, housing, wildlife, and infrastructure are all certainly part of that narrative. Other 'umbrella' areas include gender inequality, access to education, the climate crisis and environmental injustice, and systemic racism. Remember, these areas don't exist in silos, they perpetuate and exacerbate each other, and the most vulnerable in society are worst hit by broader societal injustices and inequalities. For example, climate change, pollution, and the negative impact of environmental processes and policies disproportionately impact Black people, indigenous communities, and other people of colour.

You need to understand how your cause links into the bigger picture so you have an idea of who to reach out to. I contacted UNICEF because period poverty was an obstacle to children's education the world over. I emailed the United Nations, World Vision, and the Malala Fund. I loved that Free Periods was part of something bigger, an international army of people who believed in, and were working towards, equality; who believed that a girl's education was not to be compromised and neither was it negotiable.

Remind yourself that your campaign is not an isolated quest for something huge and unattainable – it is one part of a greater fight for equality and a better world. Keeping in mind that you are one small, but crucial, person in a bigger army of activists will help spur you on and energise your activism.

Anti-racism and the importance of inclusion

Harnessing the power of inclusive and diverse activism will allow you to tap into the power of collective purpose and will add different layers of possibility to your campaign. Bringing in alternative perspectives will lift your campaign, as you'll begin to consider problems and viewpoints you may have overlooked before.

Think of it as balance, equality, and using your platform to give a voice to those who may not have the power to make themselves heard. Embracing human differences, being mindful of the language used in the everyday running of your campaign, and making sure that you recognise and acknowledge the complexities inherent in a range of experiences, are really important.

As a British-Indian woman, I have experienced racism, both casual and overt. There have been times when I have felt 'othered' in predominantly white spaces. However, I know I am privileged.

I am privileged because, among so much else, I am part of a family and group of friends who love and support me, who make me feel like there are no limits to what I can do. I live in a comfortable house in one of the most prosperous countries on earth. I went to a school that taught me to go as far as I possibly could, and now I am lucky enough to be at one of the most elite universities in the world. I am able-bodied, I haven't suffered from mental illness, and I am physically healthy. I look forward to my future and everything that is to come, and I know that there are millions who cannot say the same.

Try to think about your own privileges, and acknowledge that certain structures and traditions place you at a unique advantage in your activism. Systemic racism, the patriarchy, and the features of a capitalist society mean that those who benefit from being white male, able-bodied, having ready access to money, or having access to the internet, social media, and other resources, are implicitly privileged, at the expense of others.

The first step in your activism *must* involve 'checking' your privilege, which means admitting to the fact that certain privileges have worked in your favour, and you have received and benefited from things you have not earned. Next, think about how for others, who don't have the privileges you do, the system is stacked against them, and they need to work harder than you do to get to the same place.

Anti-racism must be a central feature of your activism, regardless of your cause. Racism can be overt or covert, and you are complicit in upholding it if you refuse to involve and uplift the perspectives of Black and minority communities in your campaigning. Let's dig deeper.

White privilege facilitates racism. Whiteness, as an ideology upon which our societal structures are built and which punctuates the culture of most of the social groups, companies, and conversations in which we all engage, needs to be actively interrogated by all of us. Regardless of race, *everyone* must work to be actively anti-racist. As activists, we are striving to carve out a better world. But what's the point, unless that world is going to be better for *everyone*?

In her book *Why I'm No Longer Talking to White People About Race*, Reni Eddo-Lodge defines white privilege as 'a manipulative, suffocating blanket of power that envelops everything we know, like a snowy day. It's brutal and oppressive, bullying you into not speaking up for fear of losing your loved ones, or job, or flat. It scares you into silencing yourself.'

She explains, 'The politics of whiteness transcends the colour of anyone's skin. It is an occupying force in the mind. It is a political ideology that is concerned with maintaining power through domination and exclusion. Anyone can buy into it, just like anyone can choose to challenge it.'

Decide to consciously challenge it in your campaign, by uplifting the voices of those who don't have the same privileges you do. Amplify Black and minority voices and acknowledge that their experiences are different to yours. Don't shy away from discomfort – embrace it. Confront the uncomfortable truths about racism and educate those who may be in denial about their own privilege or complicity in upholding racist structures.

And this really isn't something you can just ignore. To be honest, if you can choose to ignore it, that itself is a consequence of your privilege. In her excellent book *Brit(ish)*, Afua Hirsch articulates the problem with refusing to engage in this conversation by claiming not to 'see' race:

> as long as racism does exist – whether or not with a smiling face – 'not seeing race' shuts down analysis of the issue. Just because one individual chooses not to 'see race', it doesn't mean that the racialised nature of poverty, discrimination and prejudice in society at large disappears. That individual is simply refusing to acknowledge it. The effect of [this] is to deny people who do experience race – almost always members of ethnic minorities – a sense that they can have their own identity.

We all need to actively work to dismantle the biases embedded into our brains. As political activist and feminist Angela Davis says, 'In a racist society, it is not enough to be non-racist, we must be anti-racist.'

Read about racism and its systemic effects, educate yourself on the history of Black and minority communities in your country, diversify your social media feed, consciously buy from minority-owned businesses, donate to charities doing essential anti-racist work, and always call out casual racism, micro-aggressions, and racist comments online or IRL.

Centralise the perspectives of those who aren't the same as you. You can't do activism without including people of colour, those who are non-binary or from the LGBTQIA+ community, and people with disabilities. Activism *must* be intersectional and inclusive. Although it may make you feel uncomfortable, unlearning the things you've absorbed uncritically in the past is actually productive. By committing yourself to making these changes and integrating anti-racist work into your campaigning, you're enhancing your activism and fighting a better fight.

I realise that I had the luxury of campaigning for something that didn't affect me directly every day of my life. I am so lucky to say that I had no personal experience of period poverty, but I knew it was wrong and I knew it had no place in the society I want to live in. I want to live in a world where tomorrow is better than it is today, where the injustices we see right now will only ever be seen in history books in a decade, where marginalised communities are given space and agency.

The question of whether you have a right to raise awareness of issues that don't directly impact you is a big one. I've been met with hostility by other campaigners who have told me I have no right to speak about something I haven't experienced. They felt it wasn't my battle to fight. What I have always tried to do since I started Free Periods is to tell the stories of people who know what it's like to search under the sofa for coins that have fallen out of pockets and which could be exchanged for pads, of people who have felt the shame of bleeding onto their clothes when their swollen pad could not hold another drop of blood.

I am lucky that I have never felt that choking fear, but I will not stop caring about those who do. I use my place of privilege to raise the voices of others, if I can. I've always tried to be respectful of those who have confided in me about their experiences of period poverty, because I know they've trusted me. When they wanted to speak up about their experiences, I let them know I would support them, but the vast majority of them have never wanted to share what they've been through with journalists, such is the shame bound up in period poverty, and I will always honour that.

As a 17-year-old starting a campaign for the first time, I was naive about inclusivity. It became apparent very quickly that my campaigning for *girls* who suffer from period poverty was excluding an already marginalised part of society: trans men and boys, non-binary people, and gender non-conforming people menstruate too. Not everyone who had a period identified as a girl, and I was contacted by some trans boys who were hurt because they felt left out of the dialogue.

Many trans boys were living in families struggling with the cost of menstrual products and I had not thought to include them. I changed the language in the campaign straight away: all references to 'girls', I changed to 'children', and whenever I gave any interviews either over email or in the media, I was always sure to make it clear that periods happen to anyone with a womb. Many of the trans boys who had contacted me explained that they saw themselves as boys with a uterus, and feeling feminine when they menstruated made them feel fragile.

It was something that hadn't even crossed my mind. If students had to go to the nurse for free pads or tampons, I realised that this wasn't the best way to make sure that trans boys or non-binary people could access free menstrual products. So many would tell me of the crippling shame they felt in asking the school nurse or even close friends for pads when they didn't have the money to buy their own, and I understood how desperately we needed to be asking for universal access more than ever. I'd been campaigning for better education in schools around menstruation, but I knew now that that education had to be inclusive; children needed to understand that it wasn't just those who identified as girls who needed these products. I also knew that trans and non-binary students would need better support.

Tasha Bishop and I became friends just before the Free Periods protest. Tasha is the founder of The Pants Project, a non-profit organization that sells beautiful underwear to raise funds and awareness which then go on to support a number of excellent causes. She was the person who gently reminded me that not all women menstruate. Naively, in my attempt to subvert the narrative that periods are embarrassing and shameful, I had written and spoken extensively about why women needed to start embracing their period, how periods empower women by demonstrating our ability to create new life, that periods are actually incredible. Periods were still universally misrepresented and considered a taboo, even after society had made progress in so many other areas. I'd often write about how part of being a woman is to have a period.

But Tasha has Mayer-Rokitansky-Küster-Hauser (MRKH) syndrome, a condition that means she was born without a womb and would never menstruate. It affects 1 in 5,000 women. She never started her period and said that she'd felt like an outsider when her friends were discussing period stories in the school playground. As a teenager, she remembers taking red food colouring from her mum's baking cupboard and pouring the entire bottle into a pair of pants. She showed it proudly to her friends, telling them she had started her period, desperate to appear 'normal'.

I became the odd one out, and hated every single second of it, but tried to survive it by 'owning' who I was. I thought that if I pretended everything was OK, I could continue to give off the attitude that nothing fazed me and conformity was boring, and eventually I would really believe that. In actuality, I wish I'd just been able to accept how sad and broken I was by my MRKH diagnosis, because it would have saved me from years of silent suffering down the line. Then again, hindsight is a wonderful thing, and I don't think I was ready to find out at 16 that I'd never give birth, never have a period, and never have sex without an operation to build me an internal vagina. I don't think I can look back with misty eyes and wish my friends had all been trained therapists, ready to untangle my mess of gender dysmorphic, body dysmorphic thoughts, grieving the loss of a child I'd never had . . . because really, I didn't even know what was going on in my own brain, let alone anyone else's.

My mind constantly told me that I should always be a little unconventional, in order to be interesting. Weirdly, I think the blissful ignorance of being a busy 16-year-old trying to make an early-life legacy for herself, numbed me to much of the initial shock and pain of my diagnosis . . . so, maybe I'm grateful in a way, and maybe it wasn't so bad after all? Maybe humans are just better at surviving than we give ourselves credit for.

Tasha says that inclusive language really comes with listening – and then self-education. She believes that we all need to take more responsibility to be more inclusive individuals, instead of relying on the oppressed to fix their oppression themselves, and then fix 'us' as oppressors:

In an ideal world we'd all be empathic and informed enough to not marginalise anyone in the first place, but I think that's unrealistic right now.

For instance, whilst a lot of people seem to be aware that trans men get periods, there seems to be less awareness that trans women, or infertile women, or some non-gender conforming individuals don't get them – and I think that normality will come with neutrality.

Each time I've met Tasha, I've always been stuck by her self-awareness and confidence in who she is and what she stands for. I asked her how she got to that place.

It's so interesting you say that, because the main source of my anxiety comes from this ever-present sense of doom that I'm completely out of my depth, saying or fighting for the wrong thing, with an irrelevant story to share that no one cares about – and, this brings us to one of the most silent issues within activism: imposter syndrome.

My activism and feminism come from a very personal place, so in order to do my work, I separated myself from my diagnosis (even though it all revolved entirely around my diagnosis) and never truly acknowledged how traumatising it was. I think it was that separation that made me come across as confident in myself and my mission, but in truth, I think that false confidence led to severe imposter syndrome and a lot of internal anger at the world for ignoring my pain ... when I was never actually telling anyone how hurt and broken I really was, because I didn't want to sound like a bore. It was this constant rhetoric of: why am I doing this, no one's listening because no one really cares, but I can't stop because at one point this activism served me and helped me to survive, and right now it's the only opportunity to talk about my pain.

You would struggle to find activists who *don't* go through the emotional exhaustion of some form of imposter syndrome in their activism. For Tasha, it took her a long time to really understand that as long as what you have to say comes from a place of authentic passion, people will listen, and won't think you're a bore. She tells me that the secret to survival as an activist (but not necessarily conventional 'success') lies in letting go of outside validation and the disease to please, and truly connecting with the pain that fuels your fiery drive to fight for change.

Ignoring the root of your activism – which is so often pain – in order to get through the aspects of activism you most fear, will get you nowhere. In the same way that feminism serves everyone, not just women, I love that Tasha now tries to see her activism as a service to herself, not just everyone else. 'I think activists must learn that selfishness is a necessity, in the same way that empathy is.'

Talking to friends like Tasha helped me realise that I needed to think longer and harder about my choice of words and my message. I didn't want to make any group of people feel invisible or neglected in my effort to shine a spotlight and make things better for another. I needed to include everyone, and recognising that those who are hurt by a system are often best placed to think of a solution was a pivotal point in my campaigning journey. Think about who you could be excluding from your campaigning, without realising, and bring them into the core of your messaging.

It took me some time to fully engage with what my privilege meant and how it would affect my campaign. Checking your privilege forces you to be mindful and aware, recognising that you're in a position of power and responsibility if you have the opportunity to shout for change. Many others don't have the same resources or abilities, many live in countries or homes that don't encourage women to be empowered, or give opportunities to young people to engage with social or political issues.

If you're telling someone else's story, be sensitive to that, and always double-check that you're advocating with them, and not speaking for them. Within your community, be sure to include a diverse range of voices and experiences to avoid strengthening just one, single narrative and pandering to just one perspective. Include everyone – people of all genders, ages, ethnicities, sexualities, physical and mental abilities, beliefs and backgrounds – and lean in to them, so you can start listening and educating yourself. Follow social media accounts of people who couldn't be more different to you, and check who they follow. Whatever you do, don't linger within a comfortable network where everyone looks and sounds like you, agrees with you, and has similar stories to tell. Engage the most with those who are different to you, because inclusion is only going to add value and richness to your campaign.

CHAPTER 3

SPREAD THE WORD

Now you know what you want to change and how you want to change it, you need to find the best way to get your message out there. I found this tricky. I knew that I wanted to persuade the Government to provide free period products in schools, but I also wanted to get the public on board with my campaign, and try to shift society's perception of menstruation. I didn't know how to project my core message out into the world and ensure it would resonate. Quite simply, I didn't know where to start.

Let's get this straight. I'm not asking you to stand in the middle of your town and bellow maniacally into the wind, or stand at the entrance to your school with a mic and start shouting about your mission. But this part is about making some noise, and you need to do that in the smartest, most tactical way. You've got this far because you're brimming with passion and determination to make a real difference. You're here because you're not prepared to sit back anymore. So let's get your campaign seen.

Branding

When I decided to start campaigning, I hadn't quite thought everything through. The petition I was about to launch would need a logo or image to get maximum engagement from the public, and I figured that I needed a hashtag to include in the title of my petition, all Free Periods emails, social media posts, and just about everything else.

I decided on both the logo and hashtag in just a couple of hours. It makes me smile as I write this today, when I think about how far Free Periods as a brand has travelled across the globe, and how synonymous it's become with the global issue of period poverty. It makes me smile because, as I sat there on the sofa in April 2017, about to create the petition and looking online for different ideas, I had no clue what it would go on to become. In January 2020, the Prime Minister mentioned Free Periods in a speech in Parliament, after announcing that finally, every student in every school and college in England will be able to access free period products. It makes me smile because I think how little consideration I gave to the name, logo, and hashtag at first. I had no idea how critical to the campaign they would be.

Having said all of that, don't get too hung up on your branding. Ultimately, the core message and goals of your campaign are what's going to matter most. Also, your brand identity will inevitably evolve as your campaign grows and adjusts. Remember to keep it simple and flexible, and don't overthink it. Ask your friends for advice or suggestions if you're stuck, but remember that your activism, passion, and determination are far more valuable than your hashtag in getting your voice heard.

Here's what I learnt.

The name

You don't actually need to give your campaign a name. A hashtag will do, but if you want to choose a name, make it bold and make it simple. It sounds obvious, but it should be memorable and get your message across cleverly.

I started off with #FreePeriods, and then, as the campaign grew, we decided to lose the hashtag and let Free Periods stand alone as the 'brand' name. #FreePeriods was a play on words, a simple pun which nevertheless managed to suggest a lot of what the campaign was about: it worked because I was campaigning for periods to be free (free period products in all schools); it tied into the theme of schools with the idea of free periods, free time between lessons; and it tackled the shame and stigma around periods, implying that we were freeing periods, liberating ourselves from the taboo.

Don't forget to check if the hashtag is being used by other campaigns. Make sure it's going to be seen by the right people, so search for similar ones to see if they're related or similar to yours. It feels like just about every hashtag is already out there, but trust me, you'll find one that works for you if you play around and do your research. Check with family and friends to get their opinion on your shortlist. Using a hashtag is a surefire way of picking up every tweet or conversation connected to your campaign. It allows you to track what's being said, gauge opinions, and interact directly with people who are engaging with your cause.

Once you've picked your hashtag, you need to make it central to your messaging. I always tried to weave #FreePeriods into every single social media post, email, and petition update from Day 1, and then started tracking it. When you get going, ask your friends to send out just one post about your campaign from their accounts, to generate some initial traffic.

The logo

I didn't have a logo to start with, but I needed a graphic of some kind to attach to my petition. It was pretty amateur and clunky, but that's proof that you don't need to be a hotshot artist or have any sort of creative powers to come up with something that can work.

I wanted a logo that spoke to teenagers, like me, so I photo-shopped a picture of a red school canteen tray I downloaded from the internet, and placed that onto an image of a red and white checked gingham tablecloth, so it looked like a school lunch tray on a table. Then '#FreePeriods' went on top – and there it was.

I've always been shockingly bad at art, so it's quite a feat that I managed to get it looking almost decent. I went to a life-drawing class with my friends from university a while ago, mainly because they wanted to see how badly my sketch of the human form would turn out. At the end of the class, it was declared that my model looked like a walrus. My friend Meike has the picture up on the wall in her room for the days she needs a laugh.

So, even if, like me, you don't have a creative bone in your body, it doesn't matter. Keep to one or two colours that are bold and eye-catching to get across the look and feel of your campaign. I chose red, for obvious reasons.

If my dodgy artwork doesn't prove that anyone can have a go, by all means, ask for help. You could find a local artist to come up with a simple design for you, or ask someone you follow on social media to help. You could ask a talented friend, or an art student at school or college, or go directly to an art or graphic company and ask if they could do something for you. I've realised over time just how kind people can be if they understand that your intention is to do good. There are so many people out there who want to use their talents for something outside of their day to day. And remember, you don't need anything fancy at all. In fact, I would say that there's definitely a charm in something imperfect yet authentic.

Rallying support

So much of the change that Free Periods was able to orchestrate came from raising awareness and challenging our collective consciousness. It came from people hearing me banging on and on about period poverty, and constantly questioning why we were still so ashamed of our periods, for goodness' sake.

Whether you're making change at a micro-level, at school, at work, or in your neighbourhood, or if you're going bigger and hoping to effect political or policy change, you need to get your message out there.

Creating awareness can be done in lots of different ways. These are the methods I found to be most effective and the things I learnt along the way.

Petitions

In 1891, the suffragettes collected 30,000 signatures on a petition to win women the vote – it was the largest known petition of the nineteenth century, and on completion it measured 260m (850ft) in length!

When I started my campaign, I decided to start with a petition, mainly because I'd been moved to add my name to so many petitions that caught my attention. For me, it was about trying to amass as many signatures as possible in the hope that I could eventually 'deliver' it to Downing Street (100k and it *could* get debated), but it was also about throwing the issue of period poverty and the solution I'd identified out there into the world, to be seen by as many people as possible.

The #FreePeriods petition, which I started, became the backbone of my campaign. Petitions are a brilliant way of launching your mission. They demonstrate that you're not the *only* person asking for change, and that's a compelling message. There really is strength in numbers. A petition will remind you that you have an army behind you, and as you see the signatures rise, even if it's only by one person a day, you'll know you're not alone.

It shows the world that this isn't a solitary fight for change, but something much bigger, and this in itself can pile heavy pressure on brands, companies, and governments. Maya and Gemma from Our Streets Now agree:

> A petition is a great way of testing if other people care about your issue, and agree with you on the change that you want to make. Our petition gained 100,000 signatures in under 100 days, and it showed us that we had opened the lid on a problem so many people care about, and want to see change in. It's a wonderful way to show changemakers that you have support, and force them to listen.

But although a petition can be a key part of your overall strategy, it will not on its own help you to create a really powerful campaign. You need to build around it using other tools.

I remember signing the #iamperfect petition when I was 14. It was started by three women who were asking Victoria's Secret to change an advert that showed three impossibly slim models with the words 'The Perfect Body' embedded onto the image. The petition called for the brand to change the advert to something which didn't promote an unhealthy and unrealistic body image and to pledge to avoid using similarly harmful marketing in future campaigns. The petition secured over 32k signatures and successfully convinced the brand to change the caption to 'A Body for Every Body', both online and in stores, taking down the original posters and replacing them with new ones. Success!

Caroline Criado Perez threatened to see the Governor of the Bank of England in court when he announced that Elizabeth Fry, the only woman to currently feature on any English bank-note other than the Queen, would be removed when the old paper five-pound note was phased out in 2017 and new, plastic notes came into circulation. Caroline started a petition and got to work. Her message was clear. As the petition states,

> An all-male line-up on our banknotes sends out the damaging message that no woman has done anything important enough to appear. This is patently untrue. Not only have numerous women emerged as leading figures in their fields, they have done so against the historic odds stacked against them which denied women a public voice and relegated them to the private sphere – making their emergence into public life all the more impressive and worthy of celebration.

The petition secured 35,000 signatures. In 2017, the Bank of England announced that, in response to the campaign, Jane Austen would appear on the new ten-pound note. The Bank also announced that it would be reviewing the process by which they choose historical figures for banknotes, to make sure that the figures appearing are inclusive and diverse. Another success.

Caroline didn't stop there. After running through London with her dog and observing that out of the eleven statues in Parliament Square, London, not a single one of them was a woman, she also started a petition asking for a statue of a suffragette there.

There are some great men honoured, Nelson Mandela and Mahatma Gandhi among them. These are men who fought hard for their democratic and human rights and they deserve to be recognised. But where are the women who fought hard for *their* democratic and human rights? Where are the women who defied convention and police batons? Who went out on the streets? Who faced ridicule, imprisonment, violent assault, simply because they believed women were equal to men?

She campaigned relentlessly, amassing signatures over time, and finally, the Mayor of London, Sadiq Khan, agreed. If you pass through Parliament Square in London, you will see an imposing statue of a woman who fought tirelessly her entire life to secure votes for women, a woman to whom we all owe a huge debt. The statue of Millicent Fawcett casts a shadow over the grass. It deserves to be there and stands proud.

The plinth on which she stands bears the names and carved portraits of 59 women and men who fought for women's suffrage. She holds a banner inscribed with the words: Courage calls to courage everywhere. Caroline says, 'You just can't easily dismiss nearly 100,000 people.' And that's the point. When there is so much public backing, campaigns become pretty difficult to ignore.

When I ask her why she decided to start a petition, she tells me that she felt the type of change she was asking for perfectly suited a petition:

It was a single-issue campaign, a small and specific request, where there was a very clear person who was in charge of making the decision, and a very clear picture of what success looked like. A mistake I often see people make when it comes to campaigning is to assume that a petition is always the right vehicle. It isn't. A petition is the right vehicle for campaigns where there is a very clear, single ask, with a very clear, single decision-maker. A petition with a vague and complicated set of demands, and where there isn't a clear person to direct the demand at, hasn't got a hope of winning.

But it's not just campaigns with thousands of signatures that can overturn policy or generate discussion and awareness. There are countless examples of successful petitions with just a few hundred or fewer names. The key is in how you push it out – we'll come to this in a bit.

When it comes to choosing the right platform for you, there are a dizzying number of petition websites you could choose. The best way to know which is the most suitable platform for you is to visit each one and assess the pros and cons. I chose Change.org for Free Periods. There was always an email from them sitting in my inbox, either updating me on a petition I had already signed or telling me about new ones. With their huge pulling power, and very wide reach, they've hosted a number of successful, hard-hitting campaigns. There are others, including 38 Degrees, petition.parliament.uk, and iPetitions. See which one feels right for you and your campaign.

One key factor to bear in mind is whether you will be able to contact all the people who've signed your petition through the platform. This is one of the most powerful tools you have at your disposal. Even if you have only 100 signatures on your petition, having the ability to send each signer updates and make requests when *you* choose to, is really important. During my campaign, I'd send out an update when there was an exciting development, or if there was some media coverage I wanted to share.

Another area to explore is whether your petition platform

will give you the ability to liaise with a designated contact. A real human. As your campaign grows, you can take advantage of the media connections your contact has. The larger platforms have fantastic traction in some of the largest media outlets, and this is where they can be useful in supporting you and pushing out your message. Cultivate a good working relationship with your designated individual, and ask for regular calls to catch up. After I started the Free Periods petition, I contacted Rima Amin, a campaign advisor at Change.org, to ask her if she might send out an email to the hundreds of thousands of people in their database who had signed other similar petitions, in the hope that they'd also sign mine. Every time that email went out, I would watch as signatures on my petition skyrocketed. It meant that thousands more people knew about the campaign and were moved enough to spend two minutes making sure their voices were counted.

When you're setting up your petition, the onus is on you to make it as compelling as possible. This is your opportunity to outline what you're trying to achieve and why. Focus on no more than five things if you want to persuade people to sign:

1. Your petition title

This is the big, bold heading people will see when they land on your petition. The heading counts. It's got to encompass everything you're setting out to do, and it's got to be attention-grabbing and to the point. That might sound daunting, but imagine it's a banner you're taking with you to a protest – something that stands out from the crowd but gets across your aim and purpose. Make sure it's something that's easy to share on social media, too. Mine was 'Free Menstrual Products For All Children On Free School Meals #FreePeriods'. Check it can fit into the 240-character limit on Twitter: you want people to be easily able to copy the headline and paste it on social media. And don't forget to use the hashtag somewhere in the title so you can follow engagement.

Rima at Change.org tells me, 'Your petition title is your best chance to grab people's attention, so it's important to keep it clear and simple. At Change.org we recently analysed petition titles and found that the most effective used supportive first words like "save" or "protect", which include the decision-maker in the title. Our research also showed that petitions with a hashtag often get the most support.'

2. Your petition story

Why does this mean so much to you? Why you? Why now? Why is this so important for people to know about? Telling your own story, regardless of whether or not the issue has impacted you directly, or whether it's something you simply believe needs to be changed, can move and motivate like nothing else. Be honest. Be open. Draw people in by tugging at their heartstrings, using your story as a motivator, and don't hold back from telling them how this problem makes you feel. Adding some facts or statistics will always strengthen your story. Include a colourful graphic, or picture, to draw the eye – a sea of black and white is never going to hold attention for too long.

When it comes to your tone, keep it light and familiar, rather than formal and removed. You want the reader to relate to your cause and feel it, just as you do.

Remember that the first line in the petition story is the most important. It's here that people will decide if they want to carry on reading and support you, so make it as punchy as you can.

My Free Periods petition started like this: 'Millions of girls around the world are denied an education. In the UK, every girl has the right to go to school, but a growing number of them face missing school every month for the simple reason that they can't afford menstrual products. As a schoolgirl myself, I know we must change this. Period poverty must go.'

3. Your solution
Here, you need to explain exactly how this change is going to happen. What are the steps needed for things to look brighter? Be clear and to the point to hold the reader's attention.

My petition highlighted that the change had to come from the Government, particularly the Secretary of State for Education. Who is yours targeting? Is it the Government? A corporation? A shop? Your school teachers? Remember, you can change this if you get it wrong. I had to change the person my petition was targeting twice because different MPs stepped into the role of Education Secretary!

4. Your ask
This bit is really important, because although you want the person reading it to sign, you also want them to know that it goes way beyond that. Part of the allure of a petition is that it makes people feel connected and that they're part of the campaign, too.

You don't want hundreds of people to sign your petition, read your story, but forget about it the next day. Show them that this is a movement, that they're demanding change that can only happen with the collective energy and actions of *everyone*. A petition gathers lightning speed when it gets shared, so ask them to send the petition link on to five people, put the link in their Instagram bio, and post on Twitter. Add links to articles they can read, and keep the key actions in bold so they pop out.

5. *Petition updates*

As I've mentioned, choose a petition platform that allows you to update your followers. The way it works is that you can post an update and it lands in the inbox of every one of your signers. I found this a brilliant way of keeping in touch with everyone who was invested in our mission. It's a way to keep your allies close, informed, and let them know that you are all striding forwards together. Send them regularly, but not *too* regularly (people find overly persistent emails annoying!).

My first update read, 'We've hit 500!'#FreePeriods!' I was buzzing that day. I remember it clearly. It was so uplifting to know that 500 people had signed the petition, and I was desperate to say thank you. A few things to remember when you're sharing updates:

The title of the update is important. Keep it charged and attention-grabbing. Make sure it's short enough so supporters can share it on their social media. Here are some examples of the titles of my updates:

- Save the Date!!! #FreePeriods Protest on 20th December – A Protest to End #Period Poverty
- BREAKING NEWS – #TamponTax Fund is going to help end period poverty!!!! #FreePeriods
- We need YOUR help!! #FREEPERIODS
- Today is International Women's Day and we need #FreePeriods now, more than ever
- You can end #PeriodPoverty in the Budget @PhilipHammondUK!
- #FreePeriods launches new legal campaign to end period poverty!! Please support us
- Our work to get #FreePeriods for children in need and banish #PeriodPoverty is covered in The Guardian

- ACTION: Ending #PeriodPoverty in schools MUST feature in manifestos!! #GE2017 #FreePeriods

Keep your updates short. People are used to consuming content quickly, so a short, snappy message is more likely to pull them in.

Use 'We', not 'I'. Let your supporters know that there is an army of people fighting the cause, and that any progress is down to the impact of everyone working together.

Keep your updates positive. It's frustrating when you hit a wall – and believe me, you may hit several during your campaigning. While your first instinct might be to share your frustration with your supporters, your signers need to know they've lent their support to something that's got a fantastic chance of success. Be selective in the information you share and keep the tone optimistic in your updates.

Tell them you're working hard. Your signers need to know you're on it, so tell them about the work you're doing behind the scenes. Show them that this is very much a live campaign and remind them of why you're prepared to invest so much of your time on it.

Convey your passion. Don't hold back! Tell them how much this means to you, and let your drive and determination be palpable.

Just include one ask. The update is a really effective way to ask your supporters to take action, but limit it to just the one. And make it as easy as possible by telling them *exactly* what to do. It could be to:

- Come to an event, meeting, or rally you're organising.
- Ask them to send an email to a specific person asking for action.
- Tweet a particular person, the person who can make the change happen, or a particular organisation.
- Share some recent publicity the campaign has received.
- Ask them to share the petition with five other people – good if you haven't got any other useful updates to share.

Make sure your ask is reflected in the title so your supporters can readily share on social media. Remember your ultimate aim is to get traction and amass as many signatures as possible, but also to hit the right note with the right people. Take people with you on your journey. You want people to care enough about you and your cause to go one step further than you would expect.

One month after I started Free Periods, the Government announced a general election. I thought this was a brilliant time to ask all the political parties to pledge to end period poverty in their election manifestos. I sent emails and letters to my own MP, as well as every MP who'd shown interest in gender equality issues before. But I knew that this was *only* going to happen with hundreds or thousands of supporters. A petition update was the perfect way to pile the pressure on the political parties.

The update itself was brief, with a clear ask: write to your MP! I made it as simple as possible by including a template email, and included a link to a website via which MPs could be contacted directly. Easy. I was overwhelmed by the number of people who told me they had done so, and then forwarded to their friends. The proof was in the pudding, because come the time of the party manifestos being announced, every single one of the main political parties (except the one in power – not surprising) made a pledge to end period poverty. That was down to everyone who got on board. Here's the update I sent:

Hello all 6,212 of you!!

Thank you to all of you who have signed the #FreePeriods petition! We now need to work to get this included in Party manifestos. With the General Election looming, this is the perfect time to write to your MP to tell them that urgent action is needed.

It's time to end period poverty once and for all!

To get this important issue into political manifestos YOU need to write, write, write to your politicians. Period! I've drafted a template letter below. Feel free to edit, use, or ignore it as you wish.

You can send your letters to your politicians online in just a few quick steps! You can go to www.writetothem.com to find your local MPs, Councillors and MEPs. To message them, simply follow the links in the website. Once you send your message, you become a hero!

Let's make sure this election marks the end of period poverty!

Thank you!

Amika

TEMPLATE LETTER

Dear —

Every month, children across the country are missing school because they can't afford sanitary provision. This impacts on their health, education, and future life opportunities.

I have signed the petition on Change.org called #FreePeriods, which calls on the Government to take immediate action to provide free menstrual products to children on free school meals. Please see the petition here: https://www.change.org/p/theresa-may-mp-free-sanitary-products-for-girls-on-free-school-meals-freeperiods

This is an issue that the Government must address urgently, and I request that it is included in your Party's manifesto for the General Election 2017. This has already been debated in the House of Lords, and 13 MPs have signed the Early Day Motion to support these students from low-income families.

It is imperative that the issue of period poverty is tackled so we give these students the dignity they deserve, enabling them to continue their education and break out of the cycle of poverty and deprivation for themselves and future generations.

Including this campaign in your manifesto will signal an important and progressive step in including issues of gender inequality in the political agenda.

Yours sincerely,

—

Newsletters

If you haven't started a petition, or you've launched one that doesn't allow you to contact the signees, a newsletter is a really good way of developing your voice, keeping in touch with supporters and updating them on your campaign. There are plenty of platforms that offer simple, free ways to get news to a large group of people really quickly, like Mailchimp or TinyLetter, but search around to find one you like. Newsletters were a really good way to communicate before the Free Periods protest, and in the run-up to the big day, I fired off a newsletter every week to drip-feed details of speakers and sponsors. Include your logo or an image that represents your campaign every time you fire one off, so that it feels familiar when it arrives in inboxes.

You're probably wondering why we didn't put the newsletter content into a petition update instead, when we had a growing tribe of supporters whose inboxes we'd be able to land into directly? Good question, but consider whether *you* would want to be flooded by weekly updates for every petition you'd ever signed? Using newsletters, which people had actually *signed up* to receive, meant that we weren't annoying people every week. And they had the option of unsubscribing if we got super-irritating. Just make sure you don't flood the readers with information. Stick to one or two updates on your campaign and, again, one easy and simple ask.

The hardest part is getting people to opt in when the last thing they probably want is more emails in their life. You might have only your mum signing up to start with, but as your campaign grows, you'll find people are curious and want to be engaged. If you're working at a more local level, why not send around a form at school assembly, or ask your teachers to send out a request in the school newsletter? Supporters can sign up by sending an email saying they want in, they can write their name down on the form, or you could go all fancy and link a form to a Google Doc.

Getting heard

One of the toughest parts of campaigning is getting others to feel what you feel. You just *know* if others knew about your cause, if they had all the same information at their fingertips, if they felt what you feel, they would be on board, shouting into the skies. You want to pull everyone together like a huge army. In some ways, a petition does just that. But you need to cast the net out as far as you can to really set your mission in motion.

Tiara Sahar Ataii is the founder of SolidariTee, the largest student-led charity in the UK, which supports the international assistance of refugees and asylum seekers. After volunteering in Calais and Greece as a translator and interpreter with a legal aid NGO, Tiara felt compelled to continue fighting for the rights of those she had met, while raising awareness of the need for long-term, sustainable change, when she returned to the University of Cambridge to study.

She describes how important it was to educate those around her about the issue she cared so deeply about, in a specific and meaningful way. 'I didn't just want to talk about the crisis vaguely. In Greece, I had this pervasive feeling that these camps and this desperation was the embodiment of the xenophobia which plagues Europe. So I wanted to build something that would get conversations started, that would force people to challenge preconceptions.'

Her next steps changed everything. She decided to raise awareness through more than conversation – her idea was to sell T-shirts (hence the name Solidari*Tee*)! Tiara tells me:

Over £7.50 from the sale of each of our T-shirts goes to small NGOs who have a direct impact upon refugees' lives. We typically fund the most sustainable forms of refugee response, such as legal aid, although we recently offered an emergency COVID-19 grant. However, we're much more than just a T-shirt. We're also a movement – by wearing a SolidariTee on campus, you're engaging in a silent protest, and joining an international wave of student support for refugees. You're also wearing a conversation starter, allowing you to break outside of algorithms and the echo chamber.

Activism isn't just about the solitary act of feeling moved by an issue and daring to fight. It's about building a movement out of people as committed and angry as you are. Tiara tells me how she's amplified her message effectively by building a network of passionate student activists.

A key part of SolidariTee is that we're training the next generation of leaders in the refugee crisis, and showing by example that students *can* make the change that they want to see. SolidariTee is *entirely* populated by students, from our regional representatives to our board of trustees, and we've funded the entire operational expenses of three NGOs offering legal aid to refugees, reaching over 100,000 refugees and asylum seekers. If that's not proof that students can make tangible change, then I don't know what is.

To be frank, when I first started selling shirts off my bike in Cambridge, I had no idea what I was doing. But, fast forward three years, we're a registered charity, have sold over 25,000 SolidariTees, offered grants of over £300,000 to refugee aid, mobilised over 1,500 student volunteers, and have a presence in over 60 universities in the UK. I didn't receive any training for this, and for sure, I still have massive gaps in knowledge. But having the idea and the energy to carry it out is much more than half the battle.

I would also say to not be scared of failure! If the initiative doesn't work, then what you've learnt can act as the building blocks for your next venture. University is a great time to incubate projects, to widen your network, and work out how you want to contribute.

Start by making a list of people to contact who will help you raise awareness and garner support. This will get your campaign some traction. I created a Google Doc that had columns with names of journalists and the newspapers, magazines, and online platforms for which they wrote. Remember, this is something you're going to build up and out, so don't worry about including absolutely everyone who can help you right now. This is just a quick unpacking of ideas and, over time, it'll become a place where you log all your support.

Raising the profile of your campaign is built on sheer hard work, sweat, and tears. I'm not going to pretend this part was easy, or quick. It was a long and thankless task at times. Many times. There were days where I would get home from school and spend hours sending out emails from my list before tackling my homework. At the outset, I was so hopeful that each email I sent would get a response. I couldn't understand why people wouldn't respond when someone had quite clearly taken time, was brimming with passion and energy, and was ultimately just looking for a bit of help in trying to change something for the better. I couldn't have been more wrong! After a couple of weeks, I realised that sending off ten emails would elicit a response from one or two, *if* I was lucky. Sometimes there would be no response at all; that felt crushing.

People don't have time. Everyone's trying to keep it together, and to stay afloat in a rising tide of emails and to-do lists. So, when people don't reply, don't take it to heart. It's not that people don't think that what you're doing is great, just that prioritising is so hard. It can sometimes take weeks for people who are in demand to get around to responding to someone who isn't part of their immediate work, friend, or family circles. It used to get me down that it was so easy to ignore someone. But I was only 17, and didn't really know about the challenges of life, work, family, and everything else. So my advice is this:

- *Do not* let it get to you. Stay positive, optimistic, and hopeful. Know that you *will* reach the right people at the right time. Be tenacious, be patient – and whatever you do, don't stop persevering with your mission to raise awareness. Effecting change for the better is never a quick fix; it doesn't happen overnight.
- Follow up your emails with a call whenever you can. I know this sounds a bit awkward. We aren't in the habit of picking up our phones and cold calling people we've never met when we can shoot an email straight into an inbox. When I emailed someone, I would try and follow up with a call if I could get hold of their contact number online. The more I did this, the more I could see the value in it.
- Perhaps it seems a bit unfashionable, but actually speaking to someone gives you a chance to be persuasive, passionate, and human. Of course, people are unspeakably busy, but actually hearing a voice from a real-life person on the other end of the line, and forming that personal connection, is really powerful, and they're much more likely to do something from that place.

Start with those closest to you

Whatever you're trying to achieve, start by getting the support of those closest to you – look at it like ripples travelling across a pond. As the ripple spreads, the rings get wider and wider. When I started the #FreePeriods petition, I asked all my friends and family to sign, of course, and then forward to their friends. The one request I always tried to reinforce was that my family and friends ask *their* friends in turn to share with their friends, and so on.

My brother looked at me like I'd just asked him to run naked down the street when I asked him to send the petition link to his friends. He couldn't believe I was asking him to have any part to play in anything connected to periods. It took me a few weeks to convince him, but eventually he did, and I think his friends (secretly) thought the campaign was pretty cool.

I could see the signatures going up slowly, and it felt good to see that people were supporting me. In those first few days, I sent the link to everyone whose mobile numbers and email addresses I had. I personalised each message so it wouldn't sound automated, and urged them to sign, reminding them that it would take minimal time and effort (signing an e-petition can take less than two minutes). I convinced my mum and dad, and all my extended family, to send the link to all their contacts and WhatsApp groups and post it on e-bulletins at their workplaces.

I was pretty shameless and probably incredibly annoying, but I knew that I needed to build up some real interest in the campaign across different groups of people who would have different connections and spheres of influence. Someone you reach through repeated emailing could know someone critical to your campaign, someone who could really change the game, or have a pivotal idea or suggestion.

I asked my school to send out a message to all the parents, and a crafted a short email for them to pass on. Use all your groups and contacts and stay patient at this stage because you need to work outwards to widen your reach.

Find wider groups in your area

Whether you're building up support for a local campaign or delving into national or even international activism, building up local grassroots support is vital. If you know your campaign is destined for big things, and you already have influential backers, you're super lucky, but for most campaigns, including mine, this happens organically and over time.

I started to build out my campaign in the local area, asking the heads of local schools and colleges to sign my petition and talk about period poverty to break the cycle of shame and embarrassment. I reminded them it could be happening right under their noses, in their own school. I asked them to encourage girls to donate pads and tampons to food banks and hold period drives during lunchtimes.

I made a list of every school, particularly girls' schools, in my area, knowing they might just support me as a local student. Then I did some research into the schools in areas with the highest proportion of poverty and deprivation. If you've started a petition as the foundation of your campaign, emailing is more effective, so that the link to the petition can simply be clicked on to find it. A letter to an organisation like a school probably carries more weight, but the problem with an actual letter is that you're introducing the issue, then you're asking them to find the petition link themselves. Remember that in all communication, you need to try to limit the effort that people have to go to find out more, so make it easy for them.

It might be that your campaign wouldn't benefit from reaching out to schools. Every campaign will have its own core groups that the campaign leader will need get on side. Start by thinking about which groups of people your campaign will have the most positive impact on if it's successful. You might want to revisit the themes we thought about earlier, including figuring out who holds the power to make your change happen. Since the groups for Free Periods were spread across education, health, and gender, I made the following list (note that they cross over quite a bit!):

Education
Local schools and colleges
Local youth groups
Local sports groups
Local library
Charities in your area supporting young people's education
Local mentoring charity to get young people into work

Health
Local mental health charities supporting young people
Local drug awareness centres supporting young people
Youth homeless centre
Local GPs
Health centres
Local hospitals

Gender
Local feminist groups
Regional refugee centres for women

It might be that your issue doesn't transcend sectors as mine did, but that's OK.

If you're fighting for an issue, there will always be local groups you can connect with in your area who will be invested in your campaign's success and want to help. For example, if you were campaigning to persuade dog owners to pick up after their pets, you could reach out to dog walkers and send them an email with a striking poster they can hand to dog owners. Or contact vets who may be happy to leave flyers in the waiting area.

You'll have to do some research, but once you've found at least one group that's interested, you can start broadening the reach of your campaign beyond your own personal contacts and your contacts' contacts. Ask the groups you've identified to share details of your campaign on their newsletter, as well as with other groups that they're connected with.

Whether it's through a call or over email, ask them if *they* can think of other groups or organisations who might be able to support you. I established some vital connections this way.

Contact your local decision-makers

Your area will have its own decision-makers. It's really important to see if you can get them onside and start championing your cause. Even if your campaign is addressing an issue on a national level, I can't emphasise enough how critical it is to have local support.

If you're making change at a local level, this is where your core support base will be in those early days, so focus your attention here. Every area works differently in terms of how decisions are made. I wish I could be more specific and tell you who to contact, but every area in every county in every country works differently. In the UK, you can use the Government website to find the contact details of your local councillor or Member of Parliament. On the US Government website, you'll find the contact information of your senator, representative, state governor, state legislator, or mayor. Most countries will have a database of elected politicians' email addresses and/or phone numbers; you've just got to look for it!

The general rule here is to do your research, and try to find an ally at a senior level locally who can push for change on your behalf. Remember, these politicians represent *you* – don't feel intimidated about contacting them, it's their job to make change according to what voters feel is needed.

I sent an email to my local MP. In fact, over the course of my campaigning, I sent at least ten. I only ever had one reply from him and that happened when I mentioned that word that no politician likes to hear. *Protest*. It was in my email, in big, bold letters. There was a palpable media buzz in the lead-up to the protest and I suspect he was getting a bit rattled at this stage, reading about a teenager in his constituency making trouble. His response was to repeat his political party's official line word for word: schools are given money and they can decide what to do with it. A broken record.

I was really frustrated by his response, so I decided that I wasn't going to leave it there. I contacted all the local decision-makers I could. I sent emails and where I could get hold of phone numbers, I gave them a call.

I'd emailed a local councillor and my former MP, Andrew Dismore, asking for support for the campaign, and he was surprisingly quick to reply and very supportive of the campaign. He wrote a letter to Sarah Champion MP, who was the Shadow Women and Equalities Minister at the time, asking for her support, and helped circulate a press release to local and regional press. His efforts and advice were so valuable.

A really effective strategy to expand awareness of your campaign at a local level is to approach local publications sent to residents – newspapers, magazines, newsletters. Contact them directly and ask if your campaign can be included. Within the first month of starting, I managed to get Free Periods featured in two of them (I wrote a short paragraph).

One of the first publications that wrote about the campaign was a local newspaper. They are always looking to feature stories of residents doing something positive in the community, so call them and pitch your campaign. I was surprised how many people tell me, even today, that it was in their local newspaper that they first heard about Free Periods!

It's the same story with local radio. Call up your local radio station and tell them what you're doing. As with local newspapers, local radio stations are always on the lookout for local heroes and love championing the people on the ground who are working hard to make a difference.

If you're still at school, make sure you mention this, as this will provide an interesting byline and help your story to stand out from the crowd. One of the best things about local media is that they are often linked to bigger national or even international networks. The BBC has local radio stations, and there's a good chance that if they're interested in your story, you could get called up later for national radio as your details go into a much larger databank. I still get calls from national radio stations that refer to random interviews I did for small radio stations in 2017, at the beginning of my campaign. (Head over to the section on *Radio* for more tips, page 166.)

Reach national organisations

When you're ready to broaden your reach even more, and once you've got some tangible awareness of your cause, do what you did at a local level, but go bigger and even more ambitious. So, taking the three areas that I've touched upon, my national list now included the following:

Education
Teaching unions
Teaching magazines
Student unions at universities

Health
Local trusts that manage hospitals
Girls in sports charities
Pharmacy networks
Companies making pads and tampons

Gender
Fawcett Society
National Association of Women's Organisations (NAWO)
Justice for Women
Young Women's Trust

Doing the same thing, I emailed, then followed up with a call if this was possible. My request was always the same: we need to do something about period poverty, with real urgency, so please sign and share the petition and please help me get heard.

As always, most of the emails were ignored until I called someone and spoke to them personally. Once you've made a spoken connection, you have an actual human you can use as a point of contact going forward.

Not too long after starting my campaign, I noticed that there had been some recent publicity around the fact that some children who were struggling to afford pads and tampons had found the courage to go to the school nurse. And this was far from an isolated incident. In fact, a number of nurses had realised that, more and more, pupils were having to resort to asking them for pads or tampons because they weren't able to afford it, and they'd flagged this issue up with head teachers. Following my tactic of getting in touch with any and all interested groups, I contacted a magazine that went out to school nurses across the country. I'd found this by chance when searching online to see if there were some sort of association or governing body of school nurses.

I sent them an email about my campaign and asked if they could cover it. They agreed, and this was a huge boost in the early stages, because I knew that the campaign was well-received by people who were actually seeing the problem with their own eyes.

I did the same with teachers, contacting the National Union of Teachers and other teaching unions. This worked out, too, and one of the biggest teaching unions in England wrote an article about period poverty, asking their members to support Free Periods.

Securing media support and press coverage

Now you've got your core areas covered, you need to think laterally. Go big!

Think beyond the groups, publications, and organisations you've already reached out to, and make a list of every single organisation, journalist, politician, charity, magazine, and newspaper publication that could potentially cover your work. Even if you're just aiming to make change in your local area, there's every benefit to getting your cause seen by as many people as possible because this will put some friendly pressure on decision-makers.

Remember that newspaper editors are unlikely to seek you out for your story (unless you've already had some brilliant exposure elsewhere), so you need to approach them first. This bit is hard, because in the early stages of your campaign, and without the backing of any celebrity or media heavyweights shouting about your cause, you're just another campaigner trying to get some visibility. But remember that you're embarking on something important. You're doing this because you're pushing for change and devoting your time, energy, and effort to the issue because you care about our world. This is not about self-publicity or rising to fame. Hold on to the reasons why you're doing this, and they will keep you hopeful and fighting when you come up against blockades and frustrations.

Sophie Cowling is Associate Director at Freuds, the PR and communications agency widely regarded as revolutionary in the industry. The company has an established track record of purpose-led work, including launching the UN's Sustainable Development Goals in 2015 alongside Project Everyone, running meaningful campaigns, such as Comic Relief and Live 8, and working with the Mayor of London. Sophie had some insightful advice for new campaigners looking to attract media support and publicity:

- Make sure that your message is clear and easily digestible. Often these issues are way more complex than they first seem, so being able to succinctly sum up both what the issue is (even on a top line level i.e. period poverty), and what you're campaigning for (whether awareness or direct action, or both), is very important if you want to attract attention.
- Utilise your personal experience or insight, and have a perspective on the issue. The thing that differentiates your campaign from others is you, so why are *you* campaigning for this issue specifically? Have you been affected by it first-hand or seen injustice or inequality and felt like you needed to act? This insight is often key to getting media to pay attention to you and your point of view. Read opinion pieces (or op-eds, as they're known) to get a sense of how to build an argument around your point of view, which you can then present to journalists, starting with the headline statement and backed up with your evidence, insight, and experience. If it's more of

a collective campaign that you're working with others on, the same thing applies. In this instance, you want to distil multiple experiences or perspectives into a few key arguments. This personal perspective should also be reflected in your social media feed, ideally through storytelling.

- Storytelling is crucial in order to both explain the issue to those who might not know it exists (period poverty was a relatively unknown issue in the UK when #FreePeriods was launched) but also to create empathy and engagement around it, i.e. giving examples of people or things suffering as a result of this issue. If it's not something that affects individuals in their day-to-day lives, you can't assume they know it's a problem. If you can engage people through these stories, then they are more likely to remember and support your campaign.

- Create shareable and memorable pieces of bite-sized information that can be posted on your own social media platforms and which people can easily repost. This will help your messaging to travel quickly and increase the chance of it resonating with groups and individuals outside of your own direct network.

- Establishing supportive partners or alliances can be helpful in getting your message out to a network wider than your own. These can include local government, NGOs, charities, media, brands, individuals, and influencers. Their support for a campaign will help you to reach a wide audience . . . building your campaign's profile, beyond what media's able to achieve alone. You're not expected to have this network already to call upon (although great if there are leads you can pursue through friends/family) – cold approaches can often be even more effective, as it means that if they do come on board they really believe in the cause you're fighting for. This is where the importance of presenting and clarifying your argument comes back around full circle!

Publications – newspapers and magazines

Getting your cause out there though traditional print or online media will not just raise awareness of your mission, it will inform the public about what you're doing.

Research is really important here. For journalists, find those who've written about similar issues by reading articles in publications or media outlets where you'd like to be featured. Work out which journalists are writing similar stories on a regular basis or who seem concerned with your issue. If you're tackling something that's not had much publicity before, a good way to do this is to think of a broadly related issue and search online to see which journalists have cared about it enough to cover it, and who has an authoritative voice on the subject.

Check their social media to get a better idea of the issues they've covered, and check who they follow so you can approach them, too, and add them to your list. You have yourself a real coup if you can persuade a journalist who's considered a heavyweight in their field to cover your campaign. Their voice can do wonders to raise the profile of your cause and give it real credibility. Sophie tells me:

Most journalists have Twitter and Instagram profiles which are public to showcase their work; it sounds a bit stalker-ish, but you can find out quite a lot about them and their personal interests that way, be it climate, cooking, or sport, so you can best establish who might be most engaged with your story.

Work out which platforms or media outlets are the best fit to tell your story based on the content they put out already (i.e. do they profile other campaigners/activists regularly? Do they put out a lot of content on the topic you're concerned with, e.g. gender issues, the environment, climate change, etc.). Similarly, which platform's audience has the greatest crossover with the people you're trying to target? If you're trying to find out who reads VICE or *Glamour* for instance, you can go onto their websites and download their media kits (aimed at advertisers) that show their audience demographics and number of readers.

You need to be a bit strategic here. In the early stages of my campaigning, I quickly came to the realisation that key voices on women's issues in media, or on health and education, weren't showing much interest in my campaign. The most established and well-respected journalists are often those who are choked by tight deadlines and who might not have the capacity to cover a smaller campaign (even if it does have big ambitions).

I realised I had to start looking for journalists who weren't necessarily pushing out weekly articles in the biggest publications, and who weren't such big hitters. I looked for the ones who had smaller social media followings, who were perhaps new to the industry or looking for their first break. Those were the ones who were most interested in my cause, and it was from their articles and coverage that Free Periods garnered some more interest down the line. Even if only a handful of people read about you, it's about being seen by the *right* people.

Sophie echoes this:

One of the best pieces of advice I was given starting out in comms was to establish the people at the publications you'd like to cover your stories who are at a similar age or stage of their careers as you. It varies, but often the most junior writers are the ones doing the bulk of story and article writing, particularly for online publications. If you can engage them in your issue as you're starting out (even just to cover once), then as your campaign builds in momentum, they will get more senior and you will have built up a relationship with them for continued support.

If you're unsure who to contact, just as I was, write to the editor of the publications you think would take an interest in, and support your cause, or call any number you have and ask them to connect you to the news desk. They may never call you back, but some may listen, and it might pique their interest if they then see your name in their inbox later. When you send an email, choose the time you hit send carefully. Aim for Monday–Friday working hours – not at the weekend and, ideally, not before working hours. It's likely to get bumped to the bottom of the pile or passed over in favour of something else if it comes before the working day starts.

Sophie warns against pitching on a Friday afternoon, as journalists will be tying up content for the week. 'Don't pitch in the middle of a crazy news story you can see that they're covering. Be friendly! They receive hundreds of emails a day so being human, nice, and patient will always help.'

She suggests keeping the ask as concise as possible, as well as relevant and personal to the specific journalist you're contacting. Tailored approaches are definitely key to breaking through to them. Sending out mass 'bcc' emails is a definite no.

I lost count of the number of calls I made to national papers at the beginning of my campaign. I'd call up editors on the news desk (often men) and tell them about period poverty and how students were missing school because of it. Thinking back now as I write this, I suspect many of them would have preferred to hang up as soon as they heard the word 'period' – and would have done if that hadn't also been so rude. Time and again, I was met by a wall of silence, almost as though they couldn't quite believe that I'd had the nerve to call up and put them in such an uncomfortable position!

Many, many times, I asked editors or journalists if they'd be interested in covering the campaign, and I'd be told, 'No, sorry, it's not for us, goodbye.' Another thing you might hear is: 'Could you send an email please?', which is polite speak for 'I have no intention of going with this, but I just need to get you off the phone.' Don't give up. Ask them for the email address, and send them that email. If you've been persuasive and sold your campaign, they may well reconsider and forward it on to another team or contact that might be interested in covering it – this too has happened to me plenty of times.

Sophie reminds me that getting knockbacks is inevitable. Perseverance and a flexible approach is the name of the game. Trying a different journalist at the same publication, direct messaging them on Twitter (when appropriate, don't inundate!), and coming up with a new angle or rewritten pitch can all be ways of getting their attention.

> Definitely don't send repeated follow-up emails. One or two is largely deemed acceptable but you will just end up annoying them if you send any more than that! Building relationships with journalists over time does mean that they do usually acknowledge your email even if it's a 'not for us', so do try and maintain relationships with any journalists you work with along the way.

Remember that journalists are always on the lookout for new stories. That's their job. One tactic is to see if someone is looking for a story similar to yours, rather than you having to do the pitching. Follow #JournoRequests on Twitter. This is a hashtag where journalists will ask for help to find breaking stories, editorials, interviews, or quotes. You could also always post something using the hashtag asking if anyone wants to cover it.

We talked about the Global Goals earlier, the 17 Goals that could transform the world by 2030. The Goals are a great anchor for your campaign and you should definitely use all their resources online. Contact @TheGlobalGoals on social media and tell them about the work you're doing. They're always looking to raise the profile of campaigns on the ground that are looking to make our world better. Their social media account is followed by some high-profile people, as well as global organisations and UN agencies, so if they're able to lift up your campaign by giving you a shout-out, that alone is an amazing bit of publicity for your cause and mission.

Another thing you could do is contact them over email, and propose a plan that could help your campaign, or ask them to put you in touch with other organisations, working either locally, nationally, or in other countries. That's what I did, and I was able to connect with networks across the globe who were working to end period poverty.

Think of your goal as something small (or big) that is bringing us closer to a better world for everyone, as clichéd as that sounds. By standing up, grabbing the baton, and running with it, you are helping to effect change as part of a *global* movement. That's a pretty incredible thing.

Blogs and op-eds

One of the best ways to get coverage is to ask a publication or website if you can write a blog.

It's a brilliant way of putting your story down in your own words, imbued with your passion and drive. Plus, you're not expecting the media outlet to do a lot of work on it. It's a win-win for all.

I wrote blogs about period poverty for sustainable period product start-ups, for a local healthcare website, for an international charity, and for a teacher training website, among others. Sometimes, it can feel like a thankless task when you're not quite sure how many hits your article will get, but it's important to look at this as a long-term investment. Writing those blogs in the early days really helped me to clarify my thinking, and to get better at articulating the critical points that would engage people. It also meant that I was always up to date on the latest facts and figures on period poverty and gender equality, as a by-product of wanting to ensure that my arguments were relevant and current. Remember that the more you write, the more you're engaging with your topic, and the stronger your confidence and conviction becomes. This also strengthens your SEO (Search Engine Optimisation), as more mentions of your campaign online lead to increased credibility, and boost the likelihood of people coming across you and supporting the movement.

Op-eds can be game-changers. It does depend on which publication you write for, of course, but if you are successful in getting the go-ahead from a big name, it can catapult your campaign into the spotlight.

Most will ask you to write a very short pitch, which is frustratingly difficult to do. It needs to ignite interest right from the get-go – imagine how many similar pitches the editors have to deal with every single day! Getting yours to stand out from the crowd is a real challenge. I sent several pitches to national newspapers in the first months of my campaign, but I never heard anything back from them, which was disheartening.

But there are a few ways to be clever and get a foot in the door. If you've started a petition, ask your platform if they have a contact at one of the big papers. This is one of the reasons you need to cultivate a good relationship with the petition platform, and make sure they know how hard you're working on your cause.

I had a contact at the Huffington Post, so I was able to send over an article that they published as an opinion piece. I was then able to share this on social media and include a link to the piece in all my future emails. This works a treat because having one of the big players in your email to another media outlet suddenly sparks interest and curiosity. And it gives your campaign some much needed weight.

Whenever you've been covered by any publication, no matter how small, make sure you ask if they have any contacts at an even bigger publication. This is especially useful if you've got the ear of a freelancer. They often have excellent contacts in a whole network of media outlets and once you have a specific person at one of these, you're well on your way. Don't forget to mention who gave you their details, because this is what gets your email read.

I'd always dreamt of writing an opinion piece for the *Guardian*. It's a paper that's been part of the fixtures and fittings of my childhood: read by my entire family, and always strewn on a coffee table in someone's front room. I didn't get a response to my pitches to them at the start of my campaign, but I did eventually do my first piece for the *Guardian* in December 2017 – how my family rejoiced! Published the day before the protest (see chapter 4), it described the reality of period poverty, and how the shame surrounding menstruation was silencing those missing school every month. It came about by my asking a freelancer who interviewed me for a separate publication whether she knew anyone at the *Guardian*. She did, and she was kind enough to introduce me over email to a friend of hers who could help.

Celebrity and influencer backing

Sophie has secured hundreds of high-profile celebrities to back the different campaigns she's led at Freuds.

> In terms of approach, it's all about the hustle(!), not necessarily who you know. Very few people I know have ready-made celebrity or influencer networks at their disposal! As with approaching journalists, it's important to do your research to work out who your most effective campaign 'message carriers' will be. Find out who is concerned with your issue directly or has supported other causes in the past.
>
> Direct messaging should never be underestimated as a way of contacting influencers or celebrities and you may be able to get them to send you an email for their manager or publicist if you ask to be put in touch, to send more information over.

If you can find someone who genuinely supports your cause, they will almost certainly create more impactful content to raise awareness of the issue, have a vested interest in providing continued support for you, and be likely to do follow-up posts.

In my mission to spread the issue of period poverty far and wide, I knew that securing a roll call of people in the public eye with large social media followings could act as a hook to draw in members of the public who hadn't yet heard about the campaign. I started by tweeting people I thought might put their weight behind the campaign given the kind of causes they'd championed previously, and ask for a simple retweet. I'd type out something like: @_____ Please could you RT. Children are missing school because they can't afford pads. Please sign my petition for free period products in school.

Surprisingly, quite a few obliged and retweeted, and at times, there were some real spikes in the number of signs on the petition. This was exciting. The imperial force of Fame and Celebrity. Members of the public would then retweet and, overall, this generated a decent amount of traffic on the petition. I tried not to swamp my feed with requests to retweet and tried to limit it to around five people a day. It always left me baffled at how it was often those I didn't expect to engage that actually did. From celebrities like Nadiya Hussain to national institutions like the London School of Economics – these retweets helped to grow the online profile of Free Periods and attract essential supporters.

Gaining entry into that inner circle of activists with top-tier celebrity backing requires a bit of patience and a whole lot of thick skin. When I first started the campaign, I could see how much value there was in a few reasonably big names giving it a shout-out, so in my effort to be even more ambitious, I added to my list of contacts all the celebrities, influencers, and bloggers with armies of followers and undeniable clout. I searched for their agents and talent companies, called up each one, and asked if their client could support my campaign.

Most said to send an email, which I did, changing the tone of the email slightly to make it less formal and a little more emotive. At the end of the email, I'd written a few template tweets, included my faithful red canteen tray logo, and my hashtag and handle. I suggested that even if they could post on social media just once – given their crazy busy schedules – that in itself would be amazing. Some did, some didn't.

You might also want to try targeting talent agencies or publicists who represent or work with celebrities across different creative industries. I tried this, and a few of them assured me they'd send my email to the celebrities they thought might be interested in the cause, and some amazing publicity came from that.

Try getting in touch with influencers or sites that send weekly newsletters and ask them to give your campaign a shout-out. I was touched by how many influencers took the time to mention my campaign in social media posts or weekly mailshots. It might have been because I didn't stop asking and they wanted me to leave them alone, but they did it anyway.

Help Refugees has had an impressive line-up of top-tier celebrity endorsements. Josie Naughton tells me:

The most amazing people have supported Help Refugees! Never be afraid to ask! Celebrities can seem intimidating but they're just like us and they want to help. Nimko Ali, founder and CEO of The Five Foundation, which works to end female genital mutilation, had recently visited Calais and witnessed the crisis that was unfolding, particularly for the women and girls there. She invited me to the after-party for a film premiere, which Oprah was also attending. I built up the courage and waited for my moment before going over to give her a *Choose Love* bag and T-shirt, and told her how desperate the situation was on the ground. A few weeks later she was wearing it on Instagram and we raised tens of thousands of pounds from sales for partners on the ground.

Write to agents, message on Instagram, because you just never know; what do you have to lose? I would also say, always give a clear ask and easy message to get behind, don't make things complicated for people. Write the draft copy for their social media, for example, so that they can easily post it.

Don't give up

Don't get bogged down if you find you're not getting the kind of support you're after; it's often when you start to make waves in one place that people sit up and pay attention in others. Don't judge the appeal or future success of your mission on whether people you look up to are interested enough to lend you their support. It doesn't matter one bit. These are not your personal failings. You're doing something that most people don't dare to do, make time to do, or want to do.

Remember that the media is controlled by people who probably don't look like you. But in sharing your story, no matter where it gets reported, you're helping create an alternative narrative that is making its way into the spheres of power and influence, spaces that have been populated hitherto by people who are not like you. Slowly but surely, that story will start to seep into these spaces, and touch the people you least expect.

Activism is about pushing through barriers, and all the other noise competing with your voice and your message is just one of the many you're up against. You might feel, as I often did, that you're simply skirting around the edges of where you need to be to achieve your goal, and not actually being heard where it counts. But you need to be ready to play the long game if you want to see real progress. No effort is ever wasted, because if you've reached out to 50 people and penetrated the conscience of just one, you've made an impact. I've spent hours and hours firing off emails asking for someone to cover my campaign, hours writing articles in between home-work and assignments. I've stayed up until three in the morning thinking about what to do next when it felt like absolutely nothing was happening.

Dealing with setbacks is hard, but keep a laser-like focus on your goal, and whatever you do, don't stop thinking of the different approaches you can take.

It takes courage and bravery to embark upon this journey of revolt, but it takes patience and perseverance to stay the course.

Social media

Social media gets some terrible press. There are reports almost every hour about its dark side. Misogynists, trolls, and haters run rampant. The internet is awash with heart-wrenching stories of teenagers taking their own lives because of intense bullying on social media. It's led to the social media giants – Twitter, Instagram, Facebook and TikTok – being put under intense pressure to do more to protect its users. And they must. On a broader scale, Russia has been blamed for using fake news on social media to influence the 2016 American presidential election. Social networks are abused by terrorist groups like ISIS and blamed for inciting lethal vigilante attacks in India and elsewhere. It's enough to make you want to shut down every platform for good.

But when you look a bit deeper, it's clear that social media has done, and can continue to do, some extraordinary things. For every story of how destructive and damaging it can be, there's another that reminds you of what a mobilising, empowering, and downright effective force for positive change it is. Especially in the wake of COVID-19, online activism has become more crucial than ever. Despite national lockdowns and social distancing, we were able to connect virtually, continue our activism, and amplify the needs of the most vulnerable during a truly terrifying time.

If you had told the suffragettes, or Martin Luther King, that whole movements could be built off the back of 240 characters, they would have laughed.

Social media has changed the speed at which the world moves. #BlackLivesMatter grew from a hashtag into a movement that roared on social media, sparking conversations worldwide on police brutality and structural racism. #BlackLivesMatter was used almost 1.4 million times in a single day – more than five times the size of the crowd who listened to Martin Luther King give the 'I Have a Dream' speech live. (Of course, a hashtag represents a different form of activism to protesting, and the 1963 Washington March saw an estimated 250,000 people come together – impressive even by today's standards.) And then there's the #MeToo movement, which galvanised women to share their experiences of sexual harassment, and demand accountability and justice. Within 24 hours of the hashtag starting to spread, it had been used by more than 4.7 million people in 12 million posts, just on Facebook. It resulted in film producer Harvey Weinstein, a prolific sex offender, finally getting charged in 2018, then being found guilty of rape and sentenced to 23 years in prison two years later.

Suhaiymah Manzoor-Khan is a talented writer and poet. Her work interrogates history, race, knowledge and power, and she regularly educates and engages her followers through social media.

I've been able to raise awareness about and resist different narratives pertaining to Muslims, whilst raising awareness about Islamophobia and racism. We mustn't underestimate the potential of social media to educate. Whilst it can dilute our messages sometimes, I have learnt and been able to convey much through platforms like Instagram and Twitter, where knowledge can be disseminated in many forms. I've used social media to centralise a database of texts and videos for

143

people to read about White supremacy and structural racism, in light of George Floyd's murder in May 2020, and I've made educational 'explainer' videos that I share through social media.

Social media has also amplified Suhaiymah's activism, as she has applied pressure and enacted real change through the internet.

I've used social media to bring attention to causes I wouldn't have had a means or platform to do otherwise – from sharing statements about public withdrawal from events/organisations that use Counter Extremism funding to the harm of Muslim communities (Bradford Literature Festival boycott, 2019), to publicly pressurising and demanding action from the Foreign Office when thousands of British nationals were stuck in Pakistan due to COVID-19 closures. Social media democratises access and removes the 'middle man' from advocacy. Being able to speak directly, publicly, and transparently to the decision-makers whose responsibility it is to make change is uniquely possible via social media.

I honestly feel that without social media so many of us would remain silenced, deprived of platforms and communities and unaware of so much that is going on in the world. We'd also lose out on an important tool for making demands, collectivising, and coordinating material changes.

Aranya Johar is an Indian poet and feminist, who uses her social media platforms to amplify the issues she cares most about – gender equality, mental health and body neutrality. Social media has been indispensable to her activism.

I personally try to use my social media to spread awareness, to share how I educate myself, to pass the mic by sharing my platform, and to show people that changing the world can be fun sometimes but rewarding, always. The beautiful thing about being raised in this 'tech gen' (even though we often get shamed for it) is that we now have access to countless resources that can make it easier to educate others and ourselves. The internet also has the power to equalise voices. *We* pick our heroes.

Social media can humanise people. I love reading about activists who share their struggle with learning and unlearning because it is such an important side of activism that we don't often see. Identifying as a feminist doesn't mean you can suddenly let go of every patriarchal influence in your life – it's a constant journey that social media enables, by giving us the opportunity to document it.

The internet has had such a huge influence in helping people 'find' themselves. Whether it's given them the opportunity to learn more about gender and sexuality, or whether that's realising how thin shaming is *nothing* like fatphobia, I've learnt all this and more just by following and engaging with trans activists, body neutrality activists, poets of colour, and others online. Always ask *where* you're learning from, and the more diverse your sources are, the better. For example, if you're learning about caste, don't read something written by an uppercaste person like myself – dig deeper, read articles, and encourage voices that usually don't get those opportunities.

At a time where we are all living online, social media can be a lever for change. One viral tweet can virtually propel your campaign into the stratosphere. You will have no idea just how far it's gone. While I acknowledge that hashtag activism specifically has had a bad press, Free Periods was born on social media and it was social media that allowed me to speak straight into the ears of people in countries all around the globe in just seconds.

I get emails or DMs almost every day from people who've heard about Free Periods and want to get involved. Some live in towns or cities I've never heard of before, and it reminds me how brilliantly unifying social media can be.

I've never had any social media training, and my god, did I make some mistakes. But that's part of being a campaigner. You never get everything right all at once. Here's what I've learnt about how to use social media:

Start your social media accounts as soon as possible

Until I started my campaign, I had never used Twitter. I didn't know how it worked, and knew nothing about the protocol or rules. At school, my best friend Grace and I had started a lunchtime speaking programme called 'Women Who Wow'. We invited incredible women who were at the top of their game to our school to inspire the students by telling us about their own journeys to success. One of the women who came in to talk to us was Cathy Newman, a well-known TV newsreader and journalist, so just days after starting Free Periods, I reached out to her, asking her to support the campaign and spread the word. She asked me if I had a Twitter handle for Free Periods. I was embarrassed to tell her that I didn't.

Within minutes, she tweeted from her account to her huge following and put in a link to the petition. Within minutes, I could see a flurry of activity as people started adding their names to the petition in their hundreds. They were sharing their own experiences of period poverty, and were applauding the campaign for calling out the Government's inaction. It felt amazing to see how much support there was out there.

In between my schoolwork, I scrambled to create an account. I used the red tray Free Periods logo I had created for the petition as my cover photo and pinned a tweet with the petition link so it would be the first thing anyone would see when landing on my page. It was pretty basic, but it did the job. I started engaging with the masses of people who were retweeting the petition link and using the hashtag.

I'd already missed the traction of petition signers who would have followed me on Twitter if I'd had an account, which was a shame. So don't make the mistake I did – launch your social media accounts, and the hashtag, in conjunction with your campaign.

Connect with people who are engaging with your hashtag

One of the best ways of broadening your list of useful contacts who'll help raise the profile of your campaign is to look at who is actively engaging with your hashtag.

After I started my Twitter account, I'd check '#FreePeriods' to read comments and see who was liking and sharing it. Then I'd make a list of anyone who'd engaged and who could help me further, send them a DM if they followed me, or I'd find their email online and ask them if they could help more. I was bold and shameless, asking anyone and everyone I thought might have links in radio, TV, or in Westminster to help me in any way at all.

When you find just one person who backs your cause and wants to get involved, get in there quickly, especially if they're well connected and influential.

Make sure your online activism is supported by activism IRL

You can't do one without the other.

Taking the plunge from the frictionless world of social media to actually getting your hands dirty in the real world is how your campaign will really go places. Social media campaigns can mobilise entire communities as ideas travel across platforms. Protests raging around the world depend on social media to effectively broadcast their concerns and rally people in their thousands. It's doubtful whether the Women's March, Climate Change, or Black Lives Matter protests could have happened on that scale without online organisation.

But the most game-changing campaigns, the ones which people in power just can't ignore, are those where there's a flurry of activity happening on the ground, in real life. You can't change hearts and minds without offline activism. Grassroots movements have a rich history, and we can learn a lot from them. They show us that the big wins come about as a result of lots of ordinary people doing small things over a period of time. Just look at the anti-apartheid, civil rights, women's rights, and suffrage movements. Each of these have been built around face-to-face, personal contact adding layer upon layer of diplomacy and conversation. Yes, the disruptors of that time used telegrams and telephone, press or fax machines, but it was raising their voices in town squares that truly galvanised their campaigns.

We need to put effort into offline *and* online activism if we want to do more than simply raise awareness. When I started Free Periods, I spent my lunch breaks sharing stories online about period poverty, getting facts and the latest research out there to keep interest alive and people engaged. But after school, I'd be jumping on the Tube and heading into Central London, going to the House of Commons to speak with MPs and persuade them to change policy, or applying pressure on those who could, or I'd be meeting with charities or think-tanks working with the Government.

Sophie Walker says, 'Remember: petitioning and writing to people isn't a campaign – it's a useful step in building awareness and putting pressure on decision-makers. It helps you find your allies. After that, you have to get out and talk to people. Turning up in person *always* makes a difference. Looking someone in the eye can build a bond that's stronger and longer-lasting.'

It's important to apply direct pressure on people who have the power to change the status quo but aren't yet taking action, then ask your supporters to engage in a similar way online. If you know someone in power who *is* working tirelessly to champion your cause, the last thing you want is for your supporters to pile pressure on them. That's only going to irritate them. But I would post something like, 'I've just had a really productive meeting with —, and we talked about how to schedule a debate on period poverty in Westminster. Let's ask more MPs to get involved. Tweet or email your MP!!!' I'd send out a post online, or a petition update, with an example tweet and a template email for everyone to send to their own MP – a good way to apply a bit of friendly pressure on other MPs to help.

Whether it's a full-on mass protest, a school walk-out, college sit-in, or just a handful of people in your local park, taking your online campaign to the streets is one way to make sure your campaign has legs. We will look at protests more later (see page 173), but when we took to Downing Street for the Free Periods protest, it elevated the campaign to new heights.

Protests not only help supporters, who may have spread their loyalty across several causes, to invest directly in yours, but they capture hearts and minds for much, much longer. The protest marks the point at which the campaign belongs to its supporters. If they are moved enough to turn up for a protest, it becomes their mission and their fight.

We had a deluge of emails from amazing young people who came to the protest and wanted to continue to be part of Free Periods. Many of them boosted the profile of the campaign directly, by ramping up their efforts on social media, or by doing tampon collection drives, or writing to their MPs. Every piece of action taken by every single person can make change happen.

Keep it real and personal

I'm quite a private person. When my campaign took off, I wasn't ready to be thrust into the spotlight. I'll admit that, at times, I found it awkward and creepy. If you have ambitions of taking your campaign far and wide, it's unlikely that you can do this without some element of media attention. When you start campaigning, you will need to decide how much of yourself you want to reveal. It might be that you don't have a problem with sharing your private life at all. I changed my personal Instagram account to private – that was where I'd share pictures of family events, or holidays with my friends, and I didn't want that part of my life exposed.

I kept Twitter public, and learnt early on that the posts which got the most traction were the ones which were the most informal, where I spoke with my own voice. It'll be the same for you. The social media posts where you express your emotions, your horror at something, your disgust at a vile comment made about your cause, your elation at the support of someone genuinely wanting to help your campaign and so on, will be the ones that get the most engagement. Be careful about criticising named individuals, though, and remember to be kind. Always consider whether you'd be happy for the post to still exist on the internet in five, ten, or fifteen years, or whether you'd want a potential employer to find it. Express anger and don't hold your emotions back, but don't be rash.

Be you. Don't create a persona for online use, because that's just stressful, and who wants that anyway? Be honest when you share something on Instagram and write from the heart in your caption. Your followers, whether you have just a hundred or thousands, want you to be you.

Use images

You remember that line, 'A picture paints a thousand words'? Well, it's true. Our attention spans are ridiculously short. Not surprising when we face an onslaught of information every second of our lives from absolutely everywhere. Social media is a crowded space, and research tells us that tweets with an accompanying picture are 150 per cent more likely to get a retweet than those without. When people tell a story on social media using only text, anyone who's viewed that story is likely to remember just 10 per cent of it three days later. But if you pair that same story with an image, the average rises to 65 per cent.

Posting pictures of pads and tampons got the message of the campaign across, but I was sure that if people were bombarded with those same images day in, day out, they would totally switch off. By that same token, it's a good idea to try to keep your social media content varied. A great way to make sure you always have something new to post is to ask people to contribute their artwork, then build up a gallery in a Google Drive folder. Ask friends or approach a local school or art college. I asked if

I could speak about period poverty at a school, and then managed to convince the art teacher there to cover the issue of period poverty in a class. Then the students were kind enough to let me use some of their art on social media (make sure you give credit where needed), which was excellent. And at the same time, they'd also educated themselves about period poverty, engaged in conversation which helped break taboos, and wanted to help Free Periods any way they could, which was even better.

Alice Aedy is a brilliant documentary photographer, film-maker, and activist. I ask her how she's used social media and photojournalism to raise awareness of the causes she's passionate about, particularly forced migration, environmental issues, and women's stories.

> I passionately believe in the power of storytelling and I see my camera as a tool for change. Social media has allowed me to share stories from the climate and refugee crisis front-lines directly with an engaged, young audience. Not needing to rely on the traditional gatekeepers to publish my work has given me a sense of agency and freedom that I don't take for granted. Social media is also a remarkably powerful tool at my fingertips; it is the way I turn my anxiety for the future into hopeful and determined action.

Amplify the work of other activists

As activists, we should be showing up for each other IRL and online. Activism is such hard and (I will say it again) lonely work at times. A shout-out from a fellow activist feels like someone's knocked at your door to give you a much-needed hug.

If you're able to shout about another activists' work, especially if you have a larger following, it raises *their* awareness of your campaign in turn, and they may be in a position to repay that favour down the line. Even if their work isn't around a similar theme, amplifying someone else's efforts to make the world a better place makes them feel like you've got their back. They're doing something incredible, and if you, as a fellow activist, won't lift them up into the sunlight, then who will?

Encourage people to describe their own experiences so you can share them on your feed. Maya and Gemma Tutton's Our Streets Now campaign to make street harassment illegal has encouraged hundreds of girls to share their personal stories of street harassment online. This, in turn, has strengthened the campaign's message by demonstrating its urgent necessity.

Real authentic engagement with your cause online can become the beating heart of a campaign. Think about Fridays For Future, the climate strikes organised by school children across the globe. Whenever you see any posts about the weekly Friday school strikes, they're always accompanied by a retweet of pictures of youth activists holding homemade signs demanding climate action, burning in the sun or soaked in the rain. These images of total dedication and sincerity speak to the heart.

When I was at primary school, competition was a big thing. We had tests in maths and English every fortnight and after queuing up outside the headmistress's office with clammy hands, we would be told our ranking in the class. The top three were given badges to wear with pride, and we were always told to try to beat the person who came above us the next time. I hated it.

From an early age, most of us have been taught to compare ourselves with other people, to compete, and to do everything we can to win. We're encouraged to see each other as rivals, to outrun each other, to outsmart each other, to be winners, not losers. It creates a sense of fear, and that fear pushes us to compete even more aggressively. When it comes to campaigning, I think it's really unhealthy.

There isn't a finite amount of success or support out there, no one person's stock is diminished by another person's success. Someone else doing well in their efforts doesn't mean you have any less chance of getting to where you want to be. Cooperation rather than competition is the name of the game here, and I've learnt it's a valuable way to keep your campaigning positive. In fact, the more people there are campaigning for change, the more normalised and accessible activism becomes. As more of us band together and create a global army of empowered activists eliciting real change, the more likely it is that those with political power will hear our collective demands.

Public speaking

The first time I ever stood on a stage was an experience I've since packed into a box, padlocked and stored in the darkest recess of my memory. It was horrendous. Horrendous, because I'd been well and truly stitched up.

I was eight, and at primary school. We were put into pairs, told to write a poem, and given a week before we had to perform it on stage in front of the whole school. I was partnered with a boy who was out to make mischief. Let's call him Tom.

Three days into our assignment, and having already written a poem and dutifully committed it to memory, Tom told the teacher that he and I were ready to perform. That would have been fine, except that I wasn't ready. I hadn't memorised the poem, and he knew it. I'd only just finished it the night before and in my memory it was nothing but a jumble of vaguely familiar words and sentences. To make things worse, I didn't even know he'd told the teacher we were ready until we were called up onto the stage. When Tom suggested I go first, his smile widening by the minute, I should have told her I wasn't ready. I shuffled onto the stage, telling myself I could do it, that the words would effortlessly reunite in the right order and all would be well. Except my brain went black. Hot tears fell, and I muttered a few words, tried to start over again, then ran off the stage. I was mortified.

I did my first speech about Free Periods when I was 17, a few weeks after launching the petition. I had been invited to an event about menstrual equity in Central London and asked if I could make a speech about my campaign. It was to be held in the beautiful, historic chapel of the House of St Barnabas, flanked on one side by a small patch of green where workers in suits were relaxing over glasses of chilled wine in the summer sunshine. I was in the middle of my AS exams. They were spread out over several weeks and, because I had a gap of three days between papers, I decided I needed a distraction and agreed to take part.

As I got up onto the stage it felt like my heart was beating so loudly, everyone could hear it. When I spoke, I remember my voice booming around the room, bouncing off the stone walls and back into the audience. I felt tiny, eclipsed by the size of the space. I think I said everything I wanted to say, but every word felt wrong, jarring, and artificial. My passion didn't come through at all and my nerves were jangling in panic. I considered going off piste, and speaking from my heart, but I was terrified I would get tangled up in my own thoughts. I think my speech went down OK, but to be honest it's all a bit of a blur.

I remember reading somewhere that some people fear public speaking more than death or being buried alive. For most, standing exposed and alone under the spotlight of forced attention from a crowd is enough to have us trembling and stammering in a puddle of sweat, gripping the lectern like a maniac. Given my first, memorably awful experience of standing alone on a stage, I never would have thought that public speaking would become a key feature of what I do.

I've stood on stages all over the world, given a TEDx talk, spoken at the United Nations, at schools, conferences, and in front of celebrities and heads of state. My point is this: don't let any past, mortifying experience define you from this point. Not your first, not your second, third, or tenth bad experience. Leave that all behind, and know that if I can do it, so can you.

Suhaiymah Manzoor-Khan has performed nationally and internationally since her viral poem 'This is Not a Humanising Poem' went viral and gained 2 million views in 2017. On tackling the crippling fear of public speaking, she tells me,

Often the fear of public speaking is a fear of being judged, misunderstood, getting it wrong, being inarticulate, and so on. But our fear of structural violence, exclusion, deprivation of resources, persecution, and tyranny is always greater and so in the grand scheme of things, our fear to speak must not hold us back in revealing the source of larger fears.

Public speaking is a practice. No one wakes up one day and makes fantastic speeches. Instead, they start speaking and they continue speaking and over time, with practice, with embodied experience, through listening, through making mistakes, through cringing, through seeing the response or the impact – you learn. My main advice would be to lean into that fear and speak anyway.

156

Aranya Johar performed her powerful poetry for the first time at the age of 12! Since then, she's spoken in front of people like Malala Yousafzai and Emma Watson, but she's not immune to the fear either. She says, 'I get stage fright even ten years into performing, but that's because these are the responsibilities that come with being an activist and entertainer. I try to use my awareness of my stage fright to practise more. The one thing that helps to keep me grounded is knowing that I truly believe in the words I'm saying.'

When you start campaigning, the chances of your having to speak in front of more than a few people is quite high, which is great news if public speaking comes naturally to you. It may be the very first time you hear your voice take over a room, the only sound cutting through the silence. It might be the first time you've ever spoken so passionately, and you desperately want everyone else to feel what you feel too. Will they get it? Will I do it justice? Will they listen properly now or unpack it in their own time later?

Speaking in front of people is your chance to dive into their hearts and minds. It's your chance to tell them why your mission has become so important to you. You're telling people why it matters.

The more you do it, the less fear gets in the way. It might never be your favourite activity, but it may just stop being the thing that fills you with sweaty dread. Here are some tips I use to get me through it:

Speak from the heart, not from a script. The speeches which make the most impact are almost always the ones spoken without a script. That sounds scary. I get that. I'm not saying you should go in without anything at all, but see if you can speak with just a few prompts or notes.

157

This isn't for everyone – there are people who need to have memorised every word to get through it, and that's great, if it works for you. I find that having the key points in front of me as a steer is what I need most. Of course, I prep and practise beforehand, so I have a clear idea of the areas I want to cover and how I want to articulate my message.

When you're passionate about something, you *can* speak from the heart without worrying about needing a script. Ultimately, people want to see the real you, the human side, even if it's flawed and imperfect.

Firm it up with cold, hard facts. Nobody can argue with the facts. They are what they are. A few key facts peppered throughout your speech will remind people that this is real. When your speech is emotive, it can pull on the heartstrings, which is effective, but adding some hard data will drive home your message. Don't overdo the statistics, though, or it could end up sounding like a dull lecture!

Know your audience. Do some research on who your audience is going to be, so you know how to pitch the speech. At one of my first speeches, the audience consisted mainly of women in their 50s, or slightly younger. I made a reference to a Kanye West song and the blank looks on their faces still haunt me. If you're not sure what the demographic of the crowd will be, ask the organiser. If you don't know, don't mention Kanye.

Make your audience uncomfortable. You want to deliver a speech that will make the hair rise on the back of their necks. You want to own the room, but to really make an impact you need to change the way the audience think. Whatever your issue, I find that to scoop them up and bring them along with you, to really have their support, you need to confront them with the truth, and that will likely make them a little uncomfortable. Tell them why your issue is so urgent, but make sure you're clear about what you want from them and be specific about how they can get involved. What do you want every person to go home and think about? What would you like them to post or talk about after the speech? A good way to do this is to have a few key phrases you repeat throughout your speech that will really stick! Consider handing out a zine or a leaflet with some key facts, asks, and details on how people can contact you after the event.

Just because you sound nervous doesn't make it bad. Remember Oprah's #MeToo speech at the Golden Globes? It was celebrated as being both evocative and powerful, but she was almost derailed by a case of uncharacteristic nerves. Oprah admitted afterwards that one of the reasons it was so effective was because she became so nervous that her mouth went totally dry. She could barely move her lips, so she stressed each syllable just to get through it. Be like Oprah and keep it slow, so you give yourself time to think, and you're less likely to have that strange feeling of your brain and mouth not working in sync, which happens to me all the time. A case of bad nerves doesn't mean you've ruined your speech. It can show the audience just how much it means to you – and that's something nobody can teach you on any course!

Tell a story. In the summer of 2019, I was lucky enough to take part in a storytelling workshop in Johannesburg run by The Moth, and it was a revelation. In fact, it was more like a boot camp on storytelling, and it happened to be one of the best things I've ever done. There were thirteen of us, and I was the only person from outside the African continent.

159

What makes The Moth method extraordinary is that it encourages us to tell a story, without notes, without props. It asks us to be vulnerable, to be human, and to speak from the heart. We each had fifteen minutes and it was panic-inducing to stand in front of a mic, on a stage, and lay yourself open to whatever was to come. I heard personal stories that will always stay with me – of rape, of abuse, of children abandoned and loves lost.

Telling your audience your own story is what will have the room vibrating with energy, because your drive and personal mission – both essential components of your activist story – are unique. So don't hesitate in speaking your truth. It will humanise your cause and explain why *you* chose to fight for it.

Humour can also be a really effective tool in persuading your audience to get on board with your campaign. Making a 'heavy' issue light and digestible can help to educate the audience, or change their minds if they disagree with you. Grace Campbell tells me how she's used comedy to bolster her activism, subverting the traditional idea that politics consists of boring debates and speeches. 'Making people laugh as well as think can be really impactful. I've definitely found that with my work, because I mix political stand-up with quite rude feminist comedy, and my audience is usually a mix of young women and older people. Humour is a great way to "Trojan horse" themes like female masturbation and periods with the older people who need to hear it.'

Stand and deliver. You don't need to stand like Beyoncé or Wonder Woman to boost your feeling of power, but the way you stand *does* affect how confident you feel. When I get up onto a stage and look around, my instinct is to shrink into myself. I can feel it happening every time. My shoulders hunch forward and I drop my arms. But the first thing I tell myself is to breathe and stand tall, and smile. In an instant, I feel more in control, as if I own the stage.

The alternate universe. Paint a picture of what the world will continue to look like if no one takes action soon. With period poverty, the reality was that children would miss school, miss out on opportunities and their potential to be whatever they wanted to be. We were widening the gender gap by not taking action, and consigning these girls, trans boys, and non-binary students to lives of potentially permanent poverty and deprivation. Help your audience to envisage what the outcome would be if we were all to stand by and not act. Is that the kind of world they want to live in?

Imagine it's already happened and it was amazing. Psychologists often say that the trick is, before the big day, to close your eyes and imagine yourself making the speech. One thing that scares us silly before delivering a speech is the fear of the unknown and being the centre of attention. Their advice? Trick your brain into believing that tomorrow's presentation goes fantastically well. So well, in fact, that this mental rehearsal lets you start to feel all the positive emotions you want to feel ahead of the day. Hear what you will say, picture how you will stand, and see how you've captured the attention of the audience. And shout down that voice that tells you to be afraid.

Be ready for the Q & A. It's always a good idea to find out if there will be a Q & A session after your speech. Often, the floor will be thrown open and this can be unnerving – the unknown, the fear of being flummoxed by a tricky question, even not understanding the question; these can all loom large at the back of your mind while you're giving your speech.

Remember to just say you don't know if you actually *don't* know the answer to something; there's nothing wrong with that. You can't possibly have all the answers to everything, and being honest about that is perfectly OK. Simply say it's a very good question, that you'll find out the answer later and post it on social media or you'll DM the person asking if they leave their details. Just don't beat yourself up! No one will expect you to be the fount of all knowledge on everything. Try answering just part of the question if you don't have all the facts to hand. If you don't understand the question, just say. I've done this a lot, and it's fine. It's far worse to dance around an answer and be met with 'No, that's not what I meant.' Better to ask for clarification, which shows that you want to do the question justice.

Take a friend. Having someone with you at an event is the best de-stressing technique out there. I remember walking onto a stage at an International Women's Day event, in City Hall, hosted by the Mayor of London in 2018. I felt particularly nervous about it, and I can still remember how dry my throat felt.

Before the event started, I gulped down so many glasses of water that my biggest worry then became where the nearest toilet was. I was physically clenched in anxiety when I walked onto the podium, but spotting seven of my best friends in the audience was exactly the reassurance I needed. They waved and cheered and I could feel my nerves settle.

Ask a friend to film you if they can. Then, as excruciating as it is, watch yourself back and see what you can improve. I cringe watching myself, but in those early days I could see that I spoke too fast and didn't look up often enough!

Interviews

Email

Email interviews are the ones which allow you to reflect quietly on your answer in the comfort of your sitting room, bedroom, or even on the bus. Wherever you fancy, because email interviews are the most flexible form of interview. They allow you to (virtually) scrub out your answer, replace it with a better one, stop for a break, have a cup of tea, and start over.

The thing about email interviews is that when you've done one, you feel like you've done them all. They can often be repetitive, or simply different shades of each other. They can feel familiar, sometimes boring. If you've said something one hundred times before over email, you may find you're not conveying that passion as you type. Email interviews can also be the most time-consuming. A phone interview that takes ten minutes can be transposed into a three-page interview, maybe more.

Don't feel bad if you have some stock answers for email interviews. But be strategic and use the same answers only if they are going to distinctly different audiences. It will save time and a lot of energy. Or use voice notes and send them over to the journalist. Voice notes allow you to prerecord, which can take time, but it's a whole lot quicker than typing. You can tackle questions in batches and when you have the time. And you can convey your passion and emotion with your voice far better than with a sometimes flat-sounding email.

Face to face

I love face-to-face interviews. The ones where you sit down with an actual person over a coffee and a slab of cake and have a chat. At one time, this was the only way a journalist could interview, but now, given the comparative ease of email or phone interviews, these seem to be few and far between, which I think is a shame.

If you're nervous about what you're going to be asked, ask for the questions in advance, so you can have a good think about the answers before the day. A good journalist will usually know how to put you at ease and will be able to weave questions into a conversation naturally so it feels like you're having a natter with a friend. If you're not sure about something, just say you need a few seconds to have a quick think. Or if you've said something but you realise later you could have given a better answer, then just tell them. After all, the magazine, or newspaper, or whatever it is, will want the best interview from you, and if that means modifying your answers slightly, then so be it. However, bear in mind that journalists will very rarely give you approval of the text before it's published.

Broadcast interviews

Doing radio and TV interviews can be nerve-wracking. They're a bit of a double-edged sword — the good news is that you're talking to thousands of potential supporters of your campaign; the bad news is that you're talking to thousands of potential supporters of your campaign. The reach is phenomenal, and thinking about that can sometimes be panic-inducing.

My tips for doing live interviews:

- Be confident in your ability – no one knows your topic better than you.
- Know exactly how long your segment will last, so ask this in advance.

- Who is the interviewer? Listen to or watch a couple of their interviews to get a feel for their tone and views.
- Even if you're desperate to get all your points out there, don't rush it. Have just a couple of key points you want to get across, and an ask. It's better to explain a few points in detail, as this will help convince listeners of your knowledge, expertise, and commitment, than to skim over the surface of a number of points that people may have heard before or know themselves. And try to have a few key phrases that you can repeat to emphasise your goal.

I have sat in busy train stations roaring into my phone, so I wouldn't be drowned out by announcements on the overhead speakers. I've given radio interviews while on holiday because I didn't want to miss a golden opportunity (and once, I dropped my phone into a swimming pool seconds after). I've given interviews between lessons, on the H2 bus on the way home from school, and even on the train while interrailing around Europe with my friends.

I've given a quick interview five minutes after waking up, while still in bed, my voice a throaty whisper. I've tried to do it all, and whilst I would say that in the early stages, it's important to do as much as possible to raise the profile of your campaign, do not compromise on your own well-being. We'll look at this more in chapter 5.

You will know when you're doing too much at once. Take a step back and think about how you're actually feeling about it all. I started to enjoy interviews, I relished the opportunity to educate someone (especially a man!) about periods and their power. I revelled in the challenge of having a finite amount of time to get my point across. The elevator-pitch style interviews became fun. But there came a point when I realised that I was packing too much in and I knew that I couldn't be careless with my mental health. I did start to accept fewer interviews and although it was constantly on my mind that I was letting brilliant opportunities pass me by, I knew that I simply couldn't do it all. I'd find my mind whirring and I couldn't relax. You need to protect your mental health – and you need to protect it above all else, because without it, there will be no campaign. You won't have what it takes to keep going.

Now, I accept only the interviews I want to do. Saying no seems like a big thing at first. But the more that word slips out of your mouth, the easier it becomes to say. It's about guarding against burnout, protecting your confidence, and putting your needs first. And who better to know what those needs are, than you? It's about self-care, and trusting yourself to know when you've had enough. And with that trust and self-respect emerges the quiet confidence that comes from feeling in control, a feeling which can sometimes seem elusive in our lives.

Radio

It's easier to get radio interviews than it is TV interviews. Start with local radio – they'll be keen to support grassroots activists in their area, especially if your work is in the heart of the community. Call up the radio producer, whether national or local, and pitch why the show should feature your campaign and its latest developments.

If you're part of a debate, the presenter will pose a counter-argument to you, or try to stoke some controversy. I was asked to be part of a national radio call-in to talk about what I thought about the NHS agreeing to provide free period products to patients in all hospitals across the country. I hadn't done my research about the presenter. He was a middle-aged man notorious for his less than liberal views, and widely known to be inflammatory.

I was unprepared for what I was met with, while standing in my bedroom leaning against the window. While on air, he came at me with some statements, designed to provoke. His combative stance was that if female patients were to be handed out free period products in hospitals, then shouldn't male patients be offered free shaving kits? He knew exactly what buttons to push.

I reminded him that they were, already, and that was the point. Besides, having period protection was a necessity. The sum total of zero people would want female patients bleeding onto the white NHS bedsheets, I said coolly.

He wasn't having any of it. 'OK,' he asked. 'Why couldn't they ask their visitors to bring them? Why should the NHS have to provide them? Why should I pay for pads from my taxes?'

He was doing pretty well at getting my back up. But I was *not* going to lose it, even though I could practically see red mist form in front of me. I tried to stay calm, but I was muttering expletives under my breath. I didn't want to lose the audience by being equally combative, so I made my arguments calmly and was as composed as I could be. Remember that in this kind of debate, the journalist's aim will be to get some good headlines, but your aim is to raise awareness and get as many people as possible to support your mission. If they can create a bit of tension, perhaps get you to have a rant on air, then that's great for them, not so much for you. It's not easy, but remember to stay in control. You *will* get better at it. You'll be aware of the questions you're likely to be asked, and you'll learn how to bat away questions that aren't helpful to the campaign. You will learn from the mistakes you've made before, and that's as it should be. With several successful and less than successful radio interviews behind me, I've learnt that if I fluff an answer, that's actually OK. There are bigger problems in the world.

Unlike TV, radio interviews give you the protection of not being seen. Make sure you're relaxed, go into a quiet room, and make sure you're ready at least ten minutes before, in case you're on earlier than expected. Don't put the phone on loudspeaker, to minimise the possibility of picking up any background noise. I've also found that standing up always helps to make you sound, and often feel, more energetic.

TV

TV interviews take on a different dimension because unless you're an illusionist of some kind, it's hard to hide anything in front of a camera.

My first was on live daytime TV. When I heard that four-letter word 'live', I think I muttered another four-letter word under my breath. 'Live' is a big, scary word. 'Live' meant that they could ask me anything and I might not know the answer. 'Live' meant that any mess-up couldn't be cut out and filmed again. Everyone was kind, though, and good enough at their jobs to know that there was a 17-year-old in the house who looked like she might spontaneously combust in fear and panic. The presenters and I chatted away, and I soon felt at ease, which was strange because I was sitting under hot lights, flanked by a swarm of TV cameras, and I could barely see my mum smiling at me in the shadows.

The interview went fine, but it taught me a lesson. Before any TV interview, ask your contact at the TV studio for a sense of the questions in advance. It will take the edge off any anxiety you feel. They will tell you, because they want you to be excellent and they want to help you get there. At some stage, you'll have given so many interviews that you will know – but in the early stages, just ask.

Aside from the panic, there was another reason that particular interview is marked in my memory. I didn't feel like me because I was wearing way more makeup than normal and felt uncomfortable. The makeup artists were just doing their job, but my problem was that I don't usually wear very much makeup. And when I saw the person staring back at me in the mirror, it didn't look like me. I was too polite and too embarrassed to ask them to tone it down and I think it made me feel less self-assured during the interview. Now, I wouldn't think twice! After all, you need to control how you look. Nobody else is going to do that for you. Taking charge of how you look in front of the camera, and feeling good about your-self, is so important.

I did once appear on Sky News looking ridiculous. It wasn't anybody's fault, and there's sadly nobody I can blame for this particular disaster. Except maybe me, for not working out timings with precision.

I had been part of a photoshoot for the magazine i-D. The shoot was very edgy – we'd been shot in an old warehouse in East London by a well-known photographer. The shoot overran and I didn't have enough time to take off my makeup before going to the Sky studios for the news item. I ran straight onto the Tube, trying to wipe off the thick layer of green eye shadow with a wet wipe I had in my bag, but it wasn't budging. My eyes had developed some sort of irritation to the eyeshadow and started watering like I was in a full-blown weep. *All will be fine when I get to the studios*, I remember thinking. As is always the way when you need desperately to be somewhere on time, there was a signal failure and the Tube was delayed. But when I arrived and darted into the studios, I was told that because I was late, there was hardly any time for hair and makeup. Seeing my puffy eyes and tear-stained cheeks, the makeup team scrubbed away furiously to try to remove the eye shadow. It wouldn't budge. I ended up giving an international TV interview looking green and swollen, my eyes bloodshot and streaming. It's one I'll chalk up to experience.

With makeup disasters and more practice at TV interviews under my belt, I learnt to memorise key facts, quotes, and phrases. Committing them to memory means I have a bit of a security blanket in case my mind fires blanks. Data and statistics always help to back up your arguments, and, like I said earlier, you can't argue with the facts. I would often stand in front of the mirror and practise my main arguments or walk to the bus reciting some key points in my head so I could be armed with crucial evidence against the naysayers.

TV interviews can be over in a flash and often you will be left with the feeling that you never got to say what you wanted. The presenter will be interrupting you before you finish your sentence, or shaking their head rapidly to let you know you need to stop talking that minute. I learnt to deal with that, although it's pretty distracting, and you will too. Don't stop talking mid-sentence and, ideally, until you've finished what you need to say. Ask for a recording of the clip afterwards – watch it and learn from it. You will see what you could have done better, what you could have said differently, and the things you did that you can be proud of. Take all of these things, the good and the not so good, and use or adapt them for next time.

Change your wording subtly across interviews, if you can, so they don't seem too repetitive. This isn't as easy as it sounds, and I remember sitting in interviews under the warm lights in TV studios and kicking myself for using the same words and sentences, and wondering whether viewers were getting bored. Don't worry too much about repeating yourself, though, as the average viewer won't have heard every interview you've ever done, and may even be hearing your story for the first time. As I did more interviews, I stopped thinking and planning too much beforehand, and just let myself be me. I tried to speak authentically and from the heart, from a place which was unrehearsed and imperfect, because when I did, that's when I felt like I was truly connecting with the viewers. You'll discover the same thing. When you've done enough interviews that you can ad-lib a little and speak passionately in the moment, that's when you bring people into your world. That's when they feel what you feel, and they get on board with your mission. So stay open and add emotion as well as gravitas to your argument.

On the days when your confidence is rocky, and your head is full of self-doubt (who doesn't feel like that some of the time?), remember that you are here because you deserve to be here. That place is yours, and it's got your name on it. There is nobody better to create the change you want to see than you. And if you mess it up, trust me when I say it really doesn't matter. I could write a whole book about the mistakes I've made and the things I regret saying and not saying, but I am not media-trained, and I'm learning from everything I do. I don't have publicists and managers advising me how to avoid making gaffes and how to self-censor, or how to curate my arguments, who tinker with my sentences and structure my messy thoughts. I'm proud to say that I've been myself, and I've no doubt that I will make many more mistakes along the way, but I am ready for that, too.

Now is the time to start creating the future we hope for, not resign ourselves to the one we dread. And in our pursuit of that future, we – imperfect and incomplete as we are – will charge forward with our vision, our plan, our hopes and dreams of something new and better.

CHAPTER 4

MARCHING MATTERS

I still tell everyone it was the best day of my life.

The Free Periods protest, which we held within shouting distance of Downing Street on a bitterly cold December evening, was a clear sign that every setback, every trolling tweet, every terrible interview, every ignored email, had been worth it. After nine months of sitting behind my desk in my bedroom, calling out the Government's flaky commitments to ending period poverty, here I was, looking out over a sea of red and a tide of banners thrust defiantly into the inky sky. If I close my eyes, I can still feel the energy of the crowd, freezing but with anger blazing like a furnace. These people, who had brought their fury and frustrations onto the streets, were not willing to be hoodwinked anymore by false promises and hollow words. It felt like a powerful time for our generation, because suddenly, politics felt like it could be moved, shaped, and constructed by the two thousand or so people who had turned out to protest, by all of us who had got up and shown up. The old, the young, and the bloody could make things happen.

The right to protest peacefully is enshrined in Article 11 of the European Convention of Human Rights. It preserves our democratic right to gather with others and express our views collectively. Protesting in real life sends a message out to the world in a very different way to when it's done through social media. Protests build movements. Protests get results. They create the kind of power that politicians fear, sit up and take notice of. The people in authority will tell you that change only comes from within the walls of Westminster, or the White House, or from the tall office buildings that dominate our skyline. They'll tell you that you should leave it to them, that they have it all in hand, that change will come if you ask them. But they are wrong. Change comes because when we take ourselves onto the streets, we are heard. We have power, and as individuals protesting together, we can affect real and radical change.

'Exhilarating. Rewarding. Uplifting. Inspiring.' This is how it felt to play an instrumental part in a huge movement of bodies standing together in resistance and working towards the same goal. Dr Shola Mos-Shogbamimu is a lawyer, political and women's rights activist. She was a key organiser of the Women's March, one of the UK's most impactful and empowering grass-roots movements, in London in 2018 and 2019. She believes wholeheartedly in the power of protest:

> Protests are a symbol of unity and solidarity on a singular issue. They represent the collective power of the people to speak truth to power, which is absolutely essential when addressing political and social injustices. It also emboldens the silent to speak out about their experiences so that they can be used to shape a better response and solution to existing problems. It definitely fills me with awe at what people can do when we get together, put aside our differences, and bring about change.

Sophie Walker believes that the relationship between activism and more 'traditional' forms of politics has changed, as physical protesting reflects our collective energy and a roaring call for change.

Too many politicians use a politics of division – the so-called populists (who aren't popular at all) rely on stoking distrust and spreading lies to protect their own power and that of a small group of privileged people like them. Activism by comparison feels fresh and urgent – from the recent massing of young people for climate change, to the women's marches, to the coming together of communities to declare that Black Lives Matter. It feels as though, with the world in such a dreadful state, politics is trailing behind the public in understanding the urgency of the need for change.

Since COVID-19 transformed the world in early 2020, and social distancing became the norm, protesting has definitely changed. Observe physical distancing rules, stick to smaller crowds, wear a face mask, and use hand sanitiser. And think carefully about going if you have family or friends who are immunocompromised. Although it's different, protesting is still a powerful tool and definitely doesn't have to stop altogether.

For me, the Free Periods protest was like putting a bullet-proof vest onto the campaign's body. It made it stronger and impenetrable. It made it defiant and ready for just about anything. It was evidence that the real power in a campaign came from engaging offline. Just look at what's happening around the world today. Children are walking out of lessons and peacefully demonstrating on streets, in parks, and outside parliament buildings. They write history in school uniforms. They are articulate and unafraid, their passion contagious. They are showing up for each other where it counts, from Ghana to Indonesia, from Taiwan to Russia. When Greta Thunberg tells world leaders at the UN: 'You are still not mature enough to tell it like it is. You are failing us', it's a sign that the balance of power is shifting in ways we have never quite seen before.

Triggered by the brutal murder of George Floyd, racial justice protests overwhelmed the world in 2020. Globally, thousands risked their lives during a deadly pandemic, to protest against police brutality and shout about the reality of systemic racism. Statues of slave traders were pulled down, forcing governments to confront the ugly truths of their national pasts, the palpable remnants of slavery's legacy, and the distortion of colonial histories in public memory. These protests physically rebelled against centuries of oppression; the cries of young people boomed in response to the silent complicity of those who have perpetuated racism for years. Despite the circumstances, these protests reminded us of the power of physical togetherness, and the strength of collective activism.

As the throb of social media becomes the beating heart of so much campaigning, protesting in person – actually taking our bodies to the streets – is what gives a campaign legs and elevates its mission to the next level. Using signs and hashtags can shoot your cause around the world in just seconds, but I know that we never had as much news and media coverage as we did that night in December when we descended upon Westminster to make our mark.

Scarlett Curtis thinks that our generation's passion for protest shows how online activism can be elevated by gathering IRL, disproving those who might argue that social media doesn't achieve much in the political sphere. She tells me:

This isn't just 'clicktivism', it's a powerful movement. The ability for groups to congregate and protest after seeing a tweet or signing a petition shows just how powerful this generation is. We are blending online activism with huge, loud protest and both the IRL and online forms of resistance work together to create a movement that is incredibly powerful. We all really wanted to make sure that our protest wasn't just a protest but a real turning point for the Government to take action.

Organising the protest was tough, intense, scary work, but it was worth it. Neither Scarlett, Grace Campbell, nor I, had organised any kind of mass protest before and we were clueless about how to get started. What we did know was that we wanted to give people a place to vent their anger, but it had to feel positive, empowering, and inspiring. We wanted everyone who came to feel emboldened and recharged. We could sense there was something of an awakening in young people, and an intense desire to engage with the issues that were hitting them hard. I knew that from emails I'd been getting for months now, from young people who asked: 'What can I do to help?', that besides putting pressure on their MPs, they were ready to do something tangible – they just needed the signal. They were tired of being sidelined and silenced. Eight months on from starting the campaign, the time was now to shout so loud that politicians couldn't simply cover their ears.

If you're planning a protest, here are a few things that might help you.

The date

It seems obvious, but pick a date that suits your key supporters. That's not as easy as it sounds because there will always be groups of people who can't make it. Check that the date you're going with doesn't coincide with another protest, strike, or march, and make sure you're not planning it on a day where there are scheduled transport closures. Avoid religious holidays, days of big sporting events (like a major football match or a marathon), or nationwide cultural events (like music festivals). Give as much notice as you can, so the date will be marked securely in people's diaries and memories.

We decided the Free Periods protest should be on the evening of the last day of term, 20 December, the day schools in the UK ended for the Christmas holidays. This could have been genius or an epic washout, depending on whether students felt like engaging in joyful festive revolt or going home to sleep off a week of end-of-term exams. We knew there was a good chance that a lot of people would have better offers than standing and shouting while exposed to the elements – Christmas party season was in full swing after all. But it was a gamble that paid off, because, as we discovered, nothing stops a bunch of activists who are serious about making change. Not Christmas, not free booze, not even a Brexit debate in parliament.

Yes, that's right. By coincidence, once the date had been firmed up, we realised that we'd picked a day on which every single MP was going to be in Westminster for an important debate. This meant we had a golden opportunity to persuade hordes of MPs to come to the protest before or after the session in Parliament, if we were clever about it. A few weeks before, we wrote to MPs we thought would be most likely to support our calls for funding for free period products in schools, and asked them to deliver short speeches explaining why they believed period poverty had to end. As it happened, some who had politely declined that invitation approached us a day or two before the protest and asked if we had any speaking slots left, as they could see the media coverage around it was gaining momentum.

The speeches by politicians – including Jess Phillips MP, Paula Sherriff MP, Rosie Duffield MP, and Baroness Shami Chakrabarti – were truly brilliant. Even some of the politicians we couldn't accommodate with a speech came out to support us on the day, wearing woolly hats, their cheeks red with the cold.

Red tape

Sorry, but this actually is as boring as it sounds. Checking regulations is never going to be the thing you're desperate to do, but they could make or break your protest. Look online for the legal restrictions or rules you need to follow when planning your event. Ours was going to be in Westminster, so a quick Google search led us to the City of Westminster website and an application form to get the protest approved by the Metropolitan Police. It's *really* important to notify the police about your protest so that they're aware. It's also a good idea to call up your local authority (ours was the Greater London Authority), as they can let you know of any other events on the same day and give you essential information on safety precautions.

We planned to protest at Parliament Square, and all our social media, press coverage, and emails said in big bold letters: 'Come to a Period Protest in Parliament Square!!' But the day before, it became: 'Come to a period protest in Richmond Square!!!' Not quite the same alliterative impact, but it was either that or get turned away, or even arrested. Grace found out the night before the protest that we no longer had permission to be on Parliament Square. What followed was a frenzied scramble to relocate and update everyone about the new location! It was incredibly stressful. Speak to the council well in advance, and check in the run-up to the protest that everything still stands. Get the approval in writing and avoid coming out in cold sweats!

Help on the day

Having a fierce army of volunteers behind you is crucial. Scarlett, Grace and I were lucky enough to be able to build up a group of over 50 volunteers on a WhatsApp group, just made up of our closest friends and family. Everyone had a task, everyone knew where they needed to be, and everyone couldn't wait to get stuck in! From taking the speakers to a holding room (the pub), to distributing food and drink, those WhatsApp group members were the ones who kept us *all* going that night.

Create a call sheet for the day so that everyone's on the same page. Make sure to include everyone's numbers, and who to call if someone's ill or lost.

Shola agrees – organising a protest is a truly mammoth task, so you need a team!

No one person can do everything – each person will bring a different skill set to the table and, like the parts of the body, each skill is important no matter how small. It is important to remember that organising grassroots marches and protests are mostly voluntary, so people are there with a conviction to do good and they aren't paid for their time. Some will even have to juggle paid work alongside their contributions to the march/protest. It is important to respect people and their time. Tap into what they are offering and don't expect more than they're ready to give.

Speakers

A protest should be much more than a body of people marching and shouting for change. Arranging for a diverse and inclusive array of speakers who are likely to appeal to the demographic of your protesters can inspire and mobilise everyone who shows up. It adds a different dimension to the protest. At the Free Periods protest, after spending weeks approaching celebrities, influencers, and policy makers, and leveraging every single contact, no matter how tenuous the connection, we were able to secure a pretty impressive list of people who were willing to come to the protest and talk about why we needed to see change. In the end, models Adwoa Aboah, Suki Waterhouse, and Daisy Lowe all attended, together with comedians Aisling Bea and Deborah Frances-White, and other activists like Gabby Edlin, Tina Leslie, GRL PWR Gang, Chella Quint and Tanya Burr. There was even a performance by Girli.

Trust me, this wasn't easy at all. Scarlett and Grace approached everyone they knew and we begged and pleaded without shame. People in the public eye are more likely to commit if there's at least one other big name on the list, so invest in getting one or two locked down at the beginning. Even if your protest isn't going to be large-scale, it's still worthwhile finding people who are passionate about the cause to give a speech that really speaks to those who've turned out. The speakers at the Free Periods protest were fearless and bold. There was a contagious excitement that rippled through the crowd, a sense that we were on the cusp of making change. We had gathered together and we were telling the world that we were not going to be silenced.

Signs and banners

What's a protest without a banner? Not a protest. Not really.

'Make Love Not CO2' and 'Raise Your Voice, Not The Sea Level' were among other brilliant signs held up by angry students in London at one of the recent student climate change protests. Where better to see a full spectrum of placards but at our very own anti-Trump rallies during his UK visit, which gathered tens of thousands marching towards Parliament? 'Get your tiny hands off our NHS' read one, while a group of women held 'Free Melania' placards against their chests. At the Black Lives Matter rallies that took place around the world, the fury in the crowd was conveyed by clever, hard-hitting signs raised up in defiance, indicating that the fight for equality was far from over: 'Silence breeds violence', 'Respect existence or expect resistance', and 'I can't breathe', echoing George Floyd's final words, were particularly powerful.

As pictures and videos of protests are posted on social media, it's usually the banners that get the most attention, with their witty and weaponised soundbites that pack a punch.

Before the Free Periods protest, we asked if people wanted to come to a sign painting event. We thought it would be a good way of creating a little buzz before the protest itself, as well as a way to share some images online to whet everyone's appetite for what was to come. Even if it's only a few friends huddled together in someone's house to create some posters, make sure you share the images online. Try to get some publicity for the event by contacting your local paper or TV stations and ask them if they want to cover it. I will keep saying it, but you will be surprised how many people will say yes when you expect them to say no!

At the protest, my best friend Grace's 'We are not ovary-acting' went down a storm. And if we had to award prizes for the best banner, I've no doubt that 'Don't discriminate against those who menstruate' and 'Girls just wanna have FUNdamental sanitary care' would be in the Top Five.

Approach design companies and ask them if they could help create posters for the protest for free. See if any talented friends or family members could get involved. We posted on Instagram asking if anyone was willing to make posters, and at the same time, sent DMs to some incredible designers and artists whose imagery was striking, asking if they would be willing to help out.

Music

Before the day, think of a few songs and chants to belt out during the protest. You need a structure for the event, and the last thing you want is complete silence or hushed whispers, in between speeches or performances. At our protest, Grace shouted, 'What do we want?' The crowd boomed back, 'Tampons!!!' Grace shouted back: 'When do we want them?' and we all howled: 'SOMETIME THIS MONTH!!!!!' We even had some MPs joining in.

Play some music, dance, sing. Ask people on social media what songs they want to hear at the protest. Our period playlist was the backdrop to the protest. Who knew there were so many period songs out there? Here are a few, from (perhaps unintentionally) period-obsessed musicians:

(I keep bleeding, I keep, keep) 'Bleeding Love' by Leona Lewis
'Bad blood' by Bastille
'Stain' by Nirvana

183

Raising awareness

Contact PR companies who organise events. One of them may just be willing to work for free, publicising your campaign to the press and media. It's worth checking which clients they represent in the first instance. If you find companies that represent clients who are outspoken feminists or organisations that are aligned with your issue, that might be one 'in'.

A good starting point for approaching PR companies is to write down all the points you want to cover before you call them. Why are you having the protest? Why is it urgent and necessary? What have you done so far to raise awareness? How many people are you expecting to come? (That's a tough one, but be ambitious in your estimation. After all, you want as many people to turn up as possible!) What publicity are you after? I suggest calling up agencies directly because it's always more effective having contact over the phone rather than on email, when it's much easier to be ignored. It can be intimidating when the person on the other end of the phone knows nothing about your campaign, so try to educate them. Be as persuasive as you can, and let your passion come through. It's even harder to keep going when you feel they're in a rush to hang up, which is often the case, but stick to your points and make them believe that they want to be a part of it. If it doesn't work, don't worry! There are plenty of other ways you can publicise it.

Before the protest, we contacted every single newspaper, magazine, TV channel, or radio station we could think of, telling them to come and check out the event. Incessantly asking for any exposure we could get meant that in the couple of weeks leading up to the day, we saw several articles and op-eds in publications like the *Guardian*, British *Vogue*, *Glamour*, *gal-dem*, and *Metro*, urging people to attend. We were featured on podcasts, and did loads of TV and radio interviews, to try to persuade as many people as possible to come. On the day, I spent the morning at the BBC building doing live interviews for nine different stations and radio channels!

In advance of the event, you need to be as persuasive as you can when asking journalists and the media to cover it. They will have questions for you so remember to sell it! Have an email template drawn up. Here's an example of one I used:

Hi —,

I wanted to send over some info about the #FreePeriods protest. I think it's going to be a really powerful day and I wanted to ask if [publication name] could help to spread the word.

As you know, the campaign is fighting to get free menstrual products for all children in UK schools. We've spent the last month talking to a lot of politicians and political advisors and have been told this protest could be the tipping point to get this passed in parliament IF we can make enough noise!

The protest is **December 20th 5pm–8pm** and we have permission from the police to set up our stage **on Richmond Terrace opposite 10 Downing Street**. We have some really **amazing** speakers lined up (more to be announced soon – exciting!) and there's going to be a donation station accepting tampons and pads to give to homeless shelters. There will also be snacks (very important!).

You can find our website here: https://www.freeperiods.org/

Our change.org petition here: https://www.change.org/p/theresa-may-mp-free-sanitary-products-for-girls-on-free-school-meals-freeperiods

Our Instagram here: https://www.instagram.com/freeperiods/

Our Twitter here: https://twitter.com/AmikaGeorge

Our Facebook event here: https://www.facebook.com/events/1736074106702152/

And more info about the protest here: https://www.freeperiods.org/the-protest/

It would be incredible if you could come, post about it on social, and if there was anyone else you thought might want to come, to speak or help get the word out, that would be amazing. We need everyone to come together on this, and I think your voice would make a huge impact!

I've attached some very Instagrammable posters, and you can find lots more on this Google Drive.

Let me know if you need anything else!

Thank you so much!

Ami xx

Remember, if you speak to anyone, even if they say they're not interested, ask them if they know anyone else who might be. If you're contacting the local papers, remember to ask if they have contacts at national papers, and do this even if you think that nobody is likely to be interested in a small, grassroots campaign like yours (just look at how many small, local campaigners are covered in the most widely read national papers). They need to fill up their online space, and you may just be exactly what they need.

Contact publications like *TimeOut*, which broadcast event lineups, and get your protest included. Your local community can be your strongest ally, so make sure everyone in your area knows about it by putting up posters in local cafés and libraries. Ask schools if they can put the posters on notice boards, or better still, if you could give a talk in a school assembly or local town hall about why you started the campaign – and while you're doing it, mention the protest within the context of the campaign.

After our work to raise awareness, many of the journalists, radio, and TV presenters who had covered the campaign in the last couple of weeks ended up coming to the protest to check it out for themselves! On the night, and over the next few days, it was a news item across the BBC, ITV, and Channel 4, among other media outlets. Scarlett, Grace and I were interviewed countless times during the event, and journalists chatted to the protestors. Articles about the impact we had made, and what would come next, followed over the next few days. It was incredible to see so much coverage of our event, knowing that it would reach thousands more and travel many miles beyond those people who were physically there.

Social media

Thank you, WhatsApp! We couldn't have done it without you. And Facebook, Twitter, and Instagram. Social media allows internet-savvy protesters to get people out demonstrating in numbers that can't be ignored. Government-toppling shutdowns, rallies, and sit-ins have been organised with just a phone, a network, and the burning indignation that propels people out of their homes and into the streets. Our mobiles have become digital megaphones, and revolutions and rebellions in countries outside the UK have depended on social media to mobilise uprisings, with Facebook events publicising instructions about where to go and what to do. Protests are no longer coordinated in dark basements, or thrashed out in party meetings, but instead, emerge on social media, convened by smartphones and inspired by hashtags.

Scarlett says:

I think we all saw it as social media *first*, protest second. We needed to protest to show the Government that we were serious, but we needed the social media campaign to reach the maximum number of people possible. I think visuals can be a key part of a lot of campaigns, so we worked with a lot of really awesome graphic designers (like Duzi Studio) and illustrators (Alice Skinner) to design visuals that would appeal to young people and especially young girls. I have this theory of a 'three-hit approach' – you need the average person to see something three times before they really understand it and get involved, so we put a huge amount of effort into making sure the protest was being highlighted in the media, on all different kinds of social media accounts, on podcasts, and on Twitter. There were a lot of people who weren't able to make it to our protest but who really wanted to get involved with the cause, so we also gave a lot of other options for how to participate that weren't just about showing up in person.

Don't underestimate how far you can spread the word about your protest by posting about it on your social media feeds. We shared every single detail about the Free Periods protest to try to entice unsure supporters off the fence and into the streets. Our excitement was infectious, and we were constantly throwing out little teasers of what to expect, who was coming, and asking people if they wanted to be part of something big. The details were being shared around the world, by people who weren't even planning on coming. In the end, protesters turned up from as far as Cornwall, the Isle of Wight, a group even flew over from Northern Ireland! Everyone there had come because they'd seen a Tweet, Instagram story, or Facebook post publicising the event – *this* is the power of social media!

A big chunk of the protesters who turn up will only have

decided that they're coming on the day itself, and these are the ones who need a bit of friendly pressure. Creating a buzz about the event just before or on the day is a brilliant way to make that happen. What we did was to put a list together of about 40 friends and family who had a reasonable number of followers on different social media platforms. We asked them to post an event visual with the #FreePeriods hashtag along with a caption that read something like, 'Are you coming?' or, 'I'm going to be there. Are you?' They would then contact ten of their friends and ask them to do the same, and retweet the poster. On the day of the protest, #FreePeriods was the Number 1 trending hashtag on Twitter. Yes, really. That came as a result of everyone sharing, posting, tweeting, retweeting, and doing it all over again. More times than I could imagine.

Make sure that during the protest, you have a few designated people responsible for sharing photos and videos with your hashtag. Interview people who have turned out, and capture their spirit of defiance!

Post-protest plan

We created a zine to hand out to everyone after the protest, something for our fellow activists to take home with steps outlining what to do next (write to their MP, talk about periods, write about period poverty, speak at their schools, and so on). It's important to offer supporters who make it to the protest, as well as those who can't be there, a post-protest plan of action so that your uprising isn't just a passing moment and a great day out. It must serve as much, much more. Here's a letter I sent to the Secretary of State for Education the day after the protest to ask for a meeting:

Dear Justine Greening,

My name is Amika George and I'm an 18-year-old A Level Student and the founder of the #FreePeriods movement, which calls for free menstrual products for children in education.

I organised the #FreePeriods protest opposite Downing Street which took place last night.

Hundreds gathered together to send a message to you as the Secretary of State for Education, that no child should be missing school because they cannot afford menstrual products. I really hope you saw the extensive press coverage, heard the impassioned rallying cries for change, and felt the irrepressible energy from me, and all the campaigners, that are asking you to drive a change in policy.

The #FreePeriods movement is gathering momentum.

I would be really grateful if you could meet with me to discuss how we can implement this change together? I've calculated some costings, and I would very much appreciate it if you might spare some time from your busy schedule. I will be bringing my petition to Downing Street shortly, and I hope that we will soon make sure that no child misses out on their education and childhood, and that period poverty in schools is finally ended in the UK.

Best wishes,

Amika George

Although the Secretary of State for Education didn't respond, which was disappointing, the protest was a huge success. Jess Phillips MP and Paula Sherriff MP were two of the many wonderful speakers on the night, and the following week we met with them in Westminster to talk about next steps. Within three months, they'd spoken to the Minister for Sport and Civil Society, Tracey Crouch MP, who helped us to secure funding from the Government's tampon tax revenue which would be distributed to a charity working to tackle period poverty for one year. That was a huge first step.

Thanks to the protest, Free Periods was morphing into a global movement, spreading across different countries in a way I could never have imagined. Because of that, period poverty was a topic being discussed more and more in the mainstream media. When people of all ages and genders, from all backgrounds and from all regions, demand things, the power we create is electrifying. The fate of our world can be determined by citizens gathering together in public, exhilarated by solidarity. And when we fight *together*, often we win.

CHAPTER 5
PRIORITISE YOU

The night before my A-level French exam, I worked myself into a frenzied panic. I'd spent weeks, maybe months, making notes on all the topics we'd studied in class, but I still had a tower of A4 folders of vocab, quotes, and conjugations to memorise before the paper. I'd done so much prep for the exam, but I hadn't given myself enough time to funnel it all into my brain. Even more stupidly, I didn't go to bed until past 3 a.m. that night, and when I did, I was tossing and turning in a state of utter agitation and was a jittery mass of nerves until I crawled out of bed around 5 a.m. to keep pushing through my revision.

Pretty much everything that could have gone wrong in that exam did – right down to my thinking it finished half an hour before it actually did, which meant I rushed through every single question as I was flying at 90 miles per hour. It was a stupid mistake. I couldn't think straight. Reflecting on the exam later, I was convinced that in my chaotic state, I'd mistranslated the essay question and written a whole section in the wrong tense.

Slow right down

You can't do everything – that's something I've learnt very gradually. At the start of the Free Periods campaign, and in my effort to get the job done, to raise awareness and make change,

I put myself under a whole lot of pressure. In the early days, I was in a mad rush to get the word out about period poverty. After that, I was in a constant panic to keep the momentum going. I felt as though everything had to be done urgently, like, this very minute. Between my campaigning, homework, dead-lines, assignments, university applications, and just being a normal teenager, I felt utterly depleted. I would stay up most nights writing to MPs, answering interview questions over email, or writing to publications. My mum would come into my room, concerned that I was putting myself under too much pressure. But I couldn't hear it. I felt I had to keep going, as though I was trying to get to the finish line in record time.

Adwoa Aboah told me:

> There are times when I have nothing to give anyone because I've been doing so much. And I definitely think this is the case with anyone who gives themselves to activism – we often burn ourselves out. One thing that helps when I'm working and having to show up, especially with Gurls Talk, is being able to be honest about the place I'm at. I don't pretend everything is OK, I'm just totally honest about where I am. I always make sure to take time out before a Gurls Talk event because I want to give everything to the community when I'm with them.

Campaigning is rarely fast work. It's about chipping away at that structure, one piece at a time. It's about patience and grit. For me, it was three years of striving, but at the start I'd naively expected everything to move at a blistering pace. I pushed myself harder and harder, as though I was the reason for the lack of progress. *I could do better. I could do more. I could do it a different way,* I kept telling myself.

It's only now, when I look back, that I see the tiny changes which were happening on the ground. I was so preoccupied with the bigger, more visible changes, that I didn't see them. Didn't see that I was taking baby steps forward. I wanted to see a policy change so much, I had tunnel vision. I found it really hard to see or acknowledge what was happening if it wasn't clearly working towards my one main goal. But with so much coverage about periods in the media, and with conversations taking place at schools and at work about period poverty, people were starting to feel far more comfortable talking about their own experiences. I was getting email after email from supporters wanting to help. That was change, and that was progress, but I couldn't see it.

Celebrate the small wins

Realise that every *single* win matters and celebrate them all. Campaigning can be such slow, plodding work, you need to enjoy all the small wins as well as the big. The minute you think you've got somewhere, another problem rears its ugly head. Only when I started to keep a diary of all the positive things that happened every day in the campaign did I start to look at things differently. Whether it's a list of people who have asked to help, or if you feel you did a good job speaking about your work at a school assembly, or even if you feel hopeful about what you're doing, write it down and look over it on those low days when you're being too hard on yourself.

Don't limit it to your activism. Write down all the good things that happen each day. It might sound nauseatingly cheesy, but there is evidence to back this up: study after study has found a robust association between gratitude and wellbeing, including less stress and depression, better sleep and more resilience. I totally understand how this can feel like an impossible task if you're facing a daily uphill battle. No win seems big enough. But look at the tiny victories as milestones on the road, and remind yourself of them regularly. They'll help you keep going.

Be good to yourself

Looking after yourself and maintaining equilibrium in a hyper-connected world is the eternal quest. We feel guilty for prioritising ourselves, but caring about ourselves should never be considered a selfish act. Finding the balance between activism and self-care is absolutely essential. Think about it. If you're depleted, what have you got to give to other people? When you're completely spent, drained, and shattered, what good are you to anyone else? When I'm tired, you would *not* want to be around me. I start doubting myself and I become super-critical. I feel overwhelmed by just about everything, and even the smallest things morph into giant obstacles that I can't overcome.

Because activism is such intense and important work, it's exhausting. That's why we need to take ourselves out of the game every so often. Maybe you need a break for a couple of days, or even longer. I've been there. I've needed to shut everything down just to keep going.

Don't for a minute think that it's a sign that you're weak or not up to it. Instead, it reaffirms that you're strong enough to fight. Giving yourself time off shows that you have respect for your mental health, your body, and yourself, and this is what you need to energise yourself to move forward with strength. Taking a break recharges you so you can get up and start again.

Reclaim downtime by doing something you love which doesn't involve campaigning. I'll read a book, cook with my friends, go to the pub, or watch a film. And while I'm relaxing, I try to stay present, and stop my brain from meandering onto campaigning, essay deadlines, and everything else. Spend time with the people you love. Go outside. Remind yourself that you're only a small part of something much, much bigger. Think about what you do to look after other people – that's how we all need to be looking after ourselves. Cry, and let it all out if you need to. I'll admit without shame that I'm a serial sobber. Tears are a sign that I'm wiping my emotional slate clean. It's my way of unpacking the day, and I do it because I need to do it, whether I'm sad, stressed, or joyful. Nicola Mendelsohn ends every day with a hot bath, no matter where she is in the world. For her, this a key part of self-care that she refuses to compromise on; it's often her only chance to shut everything else out and to prioritise herself.

Try to learn to love time alone with nothing but the whir of your thoughts for company. Sometimes, I think we are all a bit scared to be alone and listen to our own conscience. If I'm not talking to my friends, I'm plugged into a podcast or knee-deep in a Netflix binge, immersed in someone else's life and thoughts, not my own. Don't get me wrong, I can spend a whole day watching *Friends* on loop. But now, I use the 15-minute walk to my lectures to clarify and calm my thoughts. We're all looking for distraction – time alone can feel unbearably difficult, as it means actually confronting what's going on inside you. But it's so important for your own mental health.

By contrast, Scarlett Curtis found that it was activism itself that helped her mental health – and more than anything else she tried. Activism got her out of a dark, dark place. When she discovered grassroots, feminist activism, she was 19, lonely, and depressed and living on her own in New York while attending university.

I suddenly had this beautiful community that I could be a part of and it truly gave me a reason to stay alive. We talk a lot about the risks and downsides of activism, which is definitely important, but I like to highlight the good parts as much as I can. Through feminist activism, I have found a purpose for my life, a community of friends, and a reason to get up in the morning. At a time when I didn't feel strong enough to fight for my own life, fighting for the rights of other women gave me a reason to keep going!

When I ask her how she takes care of herself as an activist, she laughs:

I never truly unplug! But I do watch a lot of TV, read a lot of books, and play a lot of Candy Crush. Yoga and the gym have helped me a lot, which is something I *never* thought I'd say. I think most activists have to live in their brains and in their feelings most of the time, and making sure I take time out every day to switch gears has truly kept me sane over the past few years. I think one of the things that has helped me most is coming to understand that all activism is a long revolution, not a quick fight. The most crucial part of this work is that you develop tools to stop you from burning out. If I work myself into the ground, I'll just want to give everything up. The change I'm looking to make is going to take decades, not years, so if I miss an opportunity or take a week off, I'm just ensuring I can keep going for the long haul.

Caroline Criado Perez suffered an unimaginable amount of vitriol, abuse, and online attacks when she started her successful campaign to get a woman on an English banknote. The relentless onslaughts that kept coming at her would have tested the most resilient of seasoned activists, and I'm keen to know how she was able to push through it every day.

I cuddle my adorable dog, do yoga when I can, and spend time with friends. I also try as far as possible not to look at it. If you stick your head above the parapet you will get pushback, it's just the reality. People who don't know you will have strong opinions on you. And there's nothing you can do about that. You just have to get on with doing what you think is the right thing to do – so campaign on things where you just can't help yourself.

After being the target of horrific rape and death threats following the success of her banknotes campaign, she has been asked several times if she would do it again, knowing what she knows now. Her answer is emphatically 'yes'. 'Not because I'm brave. But just because I literally couldn't help myself then, and I don't think I would be able to help myself now.'

Unfollow

Did you know that neither Adele, Beyoncé, nor Rupi Kaur follow anyone on Instagram? Yet we live with our faces pressed up against the virtual lives of hundreds of people, people who are really selective about what they share with the world. The problem with Instagram is that we start to see curated, manufactured images of people waking up in the morning, looking groomed to within an inch of their lives, as the norm. When the rest of us emerge from a night's sleep looking like we've gone through a tornado, seeing these unrealistic images starts to affect our self-worth. After all, how many of us can spend every summer holiday in a hammock on a beach in the Bahamas, or sip cool champagne while we sunbathe on a superyacht in the South of France? It's the worst form of peacocking there is, but we've got used to seeing these gilded lifestyles, and our brains are telling us that they're normal and we've failed because our lives don't look like that.

Why are we validated by the number of likes our photos get? Why does the approval (or lack thereof) of others dictate how we feel about ourselves on any given day? Teenagers admit to deleting photos they've posted online if they don't get enough likes.

There's growing support for the notion that Instagram can be dangerous for our mental health. It can be seen as a competitive social platform where users filter their lives to represent an ideal. There is not one person out there who looks amazing all the time, and no one is genuinely joyful, happy and living their best life every single minute of every single day. What social media does so well is that it takes the pressure we put on ourselves and amplifies it a thousand times.

Given that the average person spends almost two and a half hours a day on social media, fill your feed with the accounts that make you feel really good about you and about our world. I go through periods of cleansing my feed by unfollowing every single account that doesn't feel authentic, life-affirming and genuine, and I'll replace them with accounts of people simply doing incredible things.

Social media networks are engineered to pull you in and make it hard for you to leave, but if you're setting out to change the world, which you are, following people who are doing incredible work is uplifting, energising, and reaffirming. Instagram and Facebook are powered by algorithms that adjust what's in your feed based on what you like, who you follow, and your activity. It's scary that it kind of knows *everything*, and although you believe you're in charge, the algorithm is essentially controlling what you're viewing. So if you like and share things that are negative, or don't make you feel your best, your feed is going to put more of that sort of content in front of you. But once you start engaging with more inspiring and uplifting people, hashtags, and accounts, your feed will start to reflect that too.

Think about what you say

Back in 2019, I went on Adwoa's Gurls Talk podcast to talk about how to navigate being a teenager. I wanted to speak about having the confidence to stand up for yourself and about not caring what everyone else thinks of you. We chatted for hours, and I was so relaxed, I let my guard down and made a statement about my school friends which came out in a way that was totally different to what I had meant. When my friends heard it back and spoke to me about it, I realised how much I'd hurt them with my flippant words. I was torn up with guilt. I hated the thought that I'd made them feel they weren't important in my life, because they really were. It taught me to use words carefully, to realise that some words are powerful and can be loaded with all sorts of unintended meanings. It made me realise that what you say to two people in a room, or to a thousand, can have effects that go far beyond what you can see.

Setting boundaries

This is something I've struggled with all my life. I find it really hard to say no to anybody. Maybe some of this is down to my age, or not having the confidence to be honest with myself and brave enough to put myself first, but I've definitely got better at this over time. Setting boundaries isn't easy, and sticking to them is possibly even harder, but 'no' should be a core part of your vocab.

What I've learnt is that when you say no, you're actually honouring and respecting yourself, just as you should – and when you do that, people around you respect you more, too.

We get so used to pleasing everyone else that we start to lose sight of what our needs are, and we conflate them with the needs of others. We worry what the fallout will be from saying no, but it's better to use the energy you would have expended doing the thing you don't want to do instead to find ways to stay authentic and acknowledge that your needs matter, too.

I've realised that there are definitely ways of saying no without sounding impolite or ungrateful. Some template replies might be, 'I would love to, but I'm completely snowed at the moment. Can we check in again in the next few weeks/months? Or try, 'Thanks so much for thinking of me. Unfortunately, though, I won't be able to commit to anything right now. X is a brilliant activist, who may be able to be involved instead!' Use your lack of availability to amplify the voices of other activists or smaller organisations that might need the exposure more, or which have more time than you do. Saying no doesn't have to be a rude refusal; it can be the starting point for a meaningful collaboration or relationship, as you can suggest working on something together in the future.

I should have said no to wearing something that made me feel uncomfortable at a photoshoot for a magazine. I turned up to a studio in London one summer, and was told to wear a dress that I absolutely hated. It wasn't me at all, but I didn't say a word. I couldn't. I smiled and nodded like a puppet, dutifully wore it, and had the pictures taken. I left feeling disappointed with myself. I should have stood up for myself, but I'd been so keen to please everyone. I really felt as though I'd compromised my own integrity and let myself down.

I used to agree to every single media request, no matter how much else I had going on. In the early stages, that exposure may have been needed to create a buzz around the campaign, and you might feel the same about yours. Think carefully about how much you want to do. Just remember that whatever you decide is right for you, it's fine to say no to the things that don't interest you. Believe it or not, people *will* get over it.

And sleep on it if you're not sure. Don't rush into agreeing to do something on a whim, because (trust me, I've been there) it's ten times harder to say no once you've already said yes!

I asked Gina Martin about setting boundaries, and how to look after yourself when campaigning. She said:

There's such an internal battle to creating boundaries when your work was born from this need to connect with people and help them. I recently got to a point where my partner made me realise it was bad for me. I wasn't sleeping well because I'd answer DMs until late into the night. In the middle of the day I'd get a message about something and immediately be enveloped in reading about it, and my family and partner would lose me for hours; or I'd get a message asking for advice on a specific and tragic circumstance and I'd feel so much guilt not knowing how to respond and be sad. I still get asked daily to share campaigns, assets, surveys, ideas, products, or DMs about trials, legal battles, abusive relationships etc., but I have to draw the line because other-wise I start playing 'What cause is more important?' in terms of what I give time to or don't, which is totally unfair, and I'm not trained to give people advice.

Adwoa Aboah also recognises how imperative it is, in any form of activism, to take care of your own needs and reconnect with yourself:

Generally, I try to make sure I have the space to be by myself. I exercise and limit my time on social media, spend time with my family and friends and try as much as possible to practise what I preach by being open with everyone around me. Most importantly, I never kid myself about where I'm at, I try to be gentle, kind, and compassionate with myself. I also try to sit in and appreciate my accomplishments. It's great if everything looks wonderful from the outside, but I need to feel successful and good about myself on the inside.

Over the years I have gained such an incredible network of people around me. Especially the people I work with, they don't blow smoke up my ass, they tell me the truth. But equally they're kind, they don't add any unneeded pressure to my life, they look at me as a human, not a commodity, and they keep me grounded. Sometimes the criticism and constantly comparing myself to others through social media get to me. And even though I am so incredibly grateful for my career, there are times I don't want to be photographed, or be at the event, or have an opinion on a newsworthy topic. However, when I'm feeling negative, I always focus on the positives in my life and don't let myself get into a bad headspace. The Gurls Talk community is so instrumental in this. They always remind me of what's important – not the material things, or Instagram, or how I look, but helping others, standing for something, and feeling good about myself as a person.

Dealing with the bullies

I've heard it all. I've read all sorts of things from people saying nasty things about me, my appearance, my views, my skin colour, even my family. It's reductive, it's hurtful, it's horrible. This is the ugly side of campaigning and it's one of the hardest things to deal with. Sadly, whether we want to accept it or not, it's part of the package. But knowing how to handle it is the key to being able to lift your head high, shrug it off, and move on.

When you decide to stand up and speak out, you *will* be seen. You're here because you've chosen to do something that's going to make you stand out from the crowd, whether that's because you're the only person in your community who's said enough is enough, or whether you're going at something bigger and your face is plastered over the papers. If you're tackling a taboo subject, there are dark corners of the internet that surface from absolutely nowhere, and they will try to silence you with harassment and abuse. If you let them.

In many ways, the oppression we see of marginalised people and communities in real life is exported to social media and online spaces, where trolls can hide behind a hashtag or anonymous accounts.

I ask Suhaiymah how she deals with negativity online, and whether she responds to those who belittle her work. She says:

> I definitely don't think I have a robust approach to this yet and I still find I need to take breaks from social media and remind myself that I'm not obliged to account for other people misconstruing me or deliberately aiming to harm/ hurt me. I think a lot of the negativity I receive is not based

205

on the content of my thought and work, but on my identity and existence as a Muslim woman in the world. For that reason, I don't consider it worth responding to since there is no argument or discussion to be had – these are plain and simple attacks. I also find that not responding to online vitriol or negativity takes the wind out of people and most just give up when they don't get the reaction they want (of silencing you). However, for those persistent ones I just use the 'mute' button, which means they continue to put time and energy into their abuse and I carry on with no clue it's going on.

I also find that the support and love of online and offline communities far outweigh the impact of hate, and so I remind myself that my energies are concentrated on building community and organising for change, not defending my humanity. And sometimes the two converge when you see those who support you actually handling the racists in the comments! I have nothing to say or prove to them, so I just keep them in my prayers.

The personal comments stick, believe me. I've felt hot rage burn when I've read some pretty appalling comments directed at me online. The Centre for Countering Digital Hate's advice is: Don't feed the trolls! Its report points out that hate groups deliberately seek out engagement as a way of boosting their own profiles. When MP David Lammy retweeted some racial abuse he had received on social media, the abuser's account grew in popularity by 14 per cent. Starving the trolls of oxygen by refusing to engage with them has always been what I've tried to do when I'm met with a swell of abuse. It's the only way I can cope. It's hard, but don't rise to their toxic vitriol and don't give them the audience and attention they crave.

But what do you do when the trolls don't get bored and go away but instead keep pushing to get the reaction they're looking for? Should you spar with them? Social media companies desperately need to up their game, and it's evident that their anti-abuse tools aren't yet effective enough to protect users. Until they are, you could mute the trolls, so you don't see the tweets. That way the idiots will carry on screaming into the ether like there's no tomorrow, but nobody can hear them. You could also use Twitter's tool of hiding sensitive content so that key words are blocked. Blocking them is another way to silence them, so they can't see your account. But there may come a point when you feel that your safety is being compromised and you're being ambushed from all sides. At this stage, it's clearly harassment and that's where you need to hand it over to someone else who can protect you.

After being on the receiving end of particularly nasty online abuse, Seyi Akiwowo founded Glitch, a UK charity with the aim of putting an end to online bullying through education and campaigning. She tells me, 'No one is supporting young people when it comes to navigating the online world. Everyone assumes that because we grew up with the internet we know how to navigate it properly. Just because some of us grew up learning how to use Word Art on Windows 98 doesn't mean we know how to navigate online spaces and respond when someone says something mean to us.' To combat this, Glitch provides workshops on digital safety to women with public-facing online personas, and lobbies governments and tech companies to take action.

Worldwide, the increasing level of online abuse is staggering. Cyberbullying and online abuse is on the rise, with women being 27 times more likely to be harassed online than men. I asked Seyi what her advice would be to someone struggling with online abuse. Here are her top tips:

1. Cybersecurity

I know most of you have heard this and are probably rolling your eyes – I did. But, trust me, this is important. After a video of me speaking went viral and I suffered mob-style racist abuse, I was hacked. So invest time and resources into your online security as you would to protect your bike, car, and home. I would strongly recommend:

- Passwords for your social media and email should be long, difficult, and changed frequently. Set a regular reminder and you can use secure websites like LastPass or Yoti to store your passwords.
- Where possible, set two-step verifications on your social media and email accounts. Two-step verification asks for a code from an app or texts you a number to enter when you or someone else tries to log in to your account from an unfamiliar browser or computer.
- Familiarising yourself with privacy settings is very important. Privacy settings should be set up in such a way that you are not inadvertently sharing personal information with strangers or potential perpetrators.

2. Documenting abuse

I recommend taking screenshots of the abuse, filing them in a folder, and logging the incident in a simple table with the date, time, and site, and, most importantly, the impact it has had on you.

After my own experience, I realised there was a gap in supporting victims online. Glitch delivers training on Digital Citizenship, Digital Self-Care, and Self Defence across four continents. We offer a range of resources such as the Fix The

Glitch Toolkit and a free resource on documenting and reporting abuse.

3. Championing digital self-care

I think it's particularly important to think about your digital self-care when stepping into activism and campaigning. Self-care is not just about expensive massages and silent retreats. At its core, self-care is about identifying, communicating, and respecting boundaries. Why wouldn't this apply to digital spaces too? Define where you will be public and private, your rules of engagement online, where and how much time you will spend, and determine which types of online abuse you will respond to and how. At Glitch, we encourage our communities to communicate their digital boundaries and ask their followers, employers, membership organisations, or publicists to respect them.

Useful resources:

- Glitch: fixtheglitch.org
- Feminist Frequency: A Guide to Protecting Yourself From Online Harassment
- The Crash Override Network Resource Center
- Take Back the Tech: Safety Toolkit
- UK helplines:
  - National Stalking Helpline
  - Galop – the LGBT+ anti-violence charity
  - Revenge Porn Helpline
- You can find legal advice and solicitors online:
  - http://solicitors.lawsociety.org.uk/
  - https://www.citizensadvice.org.uk/
  - http://rightsofwomen.org.uk/get-advice/

Keep campaigning positive

From the day I started Free Periods, I decided to make my campaigning positive. I wanted to focus on the good things that were happening, rather than the bad. It was important to me that people felt good about joining the movement.

From the very beginning, there was a group of activists who didn't agree with what I was trying to do. I would see them at different events, and each time, I felt they were trying to undermine my efforts. As a 17-year-old, I was intimidated. They were much older, and far more confident and self-assured than I was. The very first time I gave a talk in public about my campaign, there was a Q & A afterwards. My petition had just got started, and I was in the very early stages of campaigning. One of the women from the other activist group was in the audience and asked me a reductive question referencing my youth, my lack of experience, the negligible support I had secured at that point. I could feel my face redden with embarrassment because here I was, trying to make some kind of change, and in front of a group of a hundred or so women, she was telling me that I couldn't do it. Later on, it became clear that they had written some articles about my campaign, questioning why I was choosing to campaign to end period poverty, something of which I had no experience. I remember wanting to retaliate, but every part of me told me not to. I think if I had, I may have changed the tone of the campaign. Not biting back and keeping the words and messages you send out positive and uplifting is a better way to draw people towards you and build up your support.

Gina Martin's mantra in campaigning is to keep things positive, simple, and informative. She told me:

Often, with big issues, we feel so deeply we want to shove the problem right in someone's face and say: 'CARE ABOUT THIS!' but I always feel like hope and positivity motivate people well, too. For my campaign, I could have said: 'I am a victim. Upskirting is horrendous and it should be against the law', but saying: 'This happened to me. It doesn't define me, but I won't let it happen the same way to someone else, so I am *going* to make this illegal on my own' is far more motivating. I also had to keep people believing the law change was possible, and I did that by only updating people and doing press when absolutely necessary (when there was some sort of action to take, or development). It's unrealistic to think the public will stay interested in an issue – no matter how important it is – in today's saturated news cycle, but by doing no media for a period while doing the heavy lifting and then popping back up with positive news, I managed to keep supporters energised.

Above all, remember that you can only advocate for others if you're looking after yourself first. There's no point in campaigning for others if you're not demonstrating compassion towards yourself and prioritising your own needs, health, and happiness. Activism starts with you – don't forget that.

END NOTE

The hardest part of activism is the decision to get started. Sitting at my breakfast table before school on an April morning in 2017, I could never have imagined how far Free Periods would go, from an online petition, to a social media hashtag, to a protest, a legal challenge, and an international movement responsible for real governmental change. You have no way of knowing how far your activism journey might take you, so make the pledge to start – that's the only way to find out.

Today, because of every person who added their name to the Free Periods petition, because of every person who refused to stay silent on period poverty, who raised their voices in defiance at the Free Periods protest, who pleaded with their MPs, who refused time and again to take no for an answer, every child in England can now access period products when they need them. Every school in the country can now access funding from the UK Government to provide these products to students for free, so no child is denied their right to an equal education. Free Periods is proof that activism really does work.

But we're not stopping there. As long as those without access to period products are denied an education, gender inequality will persist. Inspired by Free Periods, activists world-wide have now started their own campaigns to address period poverty in their countries – including countries where we wouldn't expect it to be such a prolific issue. Moving forward, I am determined to use the platform that I am so privileged to have been given, to speak out and educate, to work with organisations, charities, and legal teams around the globe to see how the work that's been done here can be rolled out in other countries.

I will continue to fight for an end to period poverty world-wide, and urge governments to recognise that ensuring free, or affordable, access to period products in schools is an investment in education, in equality, and in the future of young people everywhere.

As I write this, I'm at university, and Free Periods continues to be an integral and important aspect of my life. In between lectures, essays, and seeing my friends, I juggle emails, inter-views, speeches, and strategic plotting for our ambitious, global plan. Stretching our aim to end period poverty globally, while tackling the period shame and taboo, won't be an easy task. The work that lies ahead will be slow and tedious, draining and repetitive, but the impact of activism will always outweigh its drawbacks.

Without a doubt, campaigning has enriched my life in a way I struggle to put into words. It's been enriched by the hope, experience, and friendship of all the people who've trusted me with their stories; by all the people who gave me a voice, who lifted me up, who listened, who created space for me, who helped me to believe that I could actually make a difference.

I truly believe that you can too. But the first step is deciding to begin. It is refusing to allow injustice and inequalities to pass you by. It is deciding to be the person who demands something different.

Campaigning is not something you embark on because it looks like a laugh, or because you have a bit of spare time, or you need a new challenge for a new year. It comes from some-where deep within. From a flicker of hope that things can be better and from believing that we all have a part to play in making it happen. From seeing a world which is battered and bruised by the complacency and denial of world leaders, from listening to their talk of progress as slow and steady change, when all we hear is the constant thumping of a ticking clock. From seeing fascists win elections and terrorist groups kill and maim, from knowing that not one single country on the planet has achieved gender equality, and that the perpetual reality of racism systematically disadvantages Black and minority communities.

Campaigning starts with hope. Hope is believing that the world can be better. It is seeing heroes in the shape of young people, red, raging, and raw, taking to the streets and shifting the balance of power, rewriting what is possible and changing the rules. It starts from fighting the small fires that everybody has overlooked. From knowing you may get scorched, but you do it anyway.

If you're the kind of person who can imagine a more equal, more peaceful world, who will refuse to be silenced, and will keep going even when the future looks bleak and the work feels futile, then you're ready to go. All you have to do is start.

TIMELINE

April 2017

After reading an article about girls in the UK missing school due to period poverty, I start the Free Periods petition from my bedroom in North London. In a couple of weeks, it gains over 2,000 signatures.

May 2017

After I reach out to all UK political parties ahead of the 2017 election, the Green Party and the Women's Equality Party pledge to end period poverty in their election manifestos. This marks the first mention of periods from any political party in the run-up to the general election. Soon, the Liberal Democrat Party incorporate a similar pledge to end period poverty in their manifesto too.

September 2017

The Labour Party pledge £10m to tackle period poverty in the UK if they come to power.

November 2017

I deliver a TEDx talk in London, entitled 'Period Poverty: Breaking the Silence'.

December 2017

Free Periods joins forces with The Pink Protest to stage a peaceful protest outside Downing Street. Over 2,000 people come, and speakers include Adwoa Aboah, Aisling Bea, Suki Waterhouse, Jess Phillips MP, and Tanya Burr.

March 2018

After considerable pressure, the Government pledges £1.5m of funding to tackle period poverty in the UK.

September 2018

I receive the Campaign Award at Goalkeepers, New York, from Bill and Melinda Gates and the United Nations. Free Periods is propelled into the global spotlight.

I'm able to speak about period poverty with a global focus, highlighting the immediate need for international governments to take action.

November 2018

Free Periods becomes a limited company with a Board of Directors, in advance of the legal challenge to the Government.

January 2019

Free Periods joins forces with the Red Box Project to launch a legal campaign to challenge the Government, working with the legal firm Hausfeld, and barristers Schona Jolly QC and Claire McCann from Cloisters chambers.

Free Periods' aim is to persuade the Government to comply with its existing obligations under the Equality Act 2010 to ensure that all children have equal access to their education, by the provision of free menstrual products in all schools and colleges.

March 2019 – VICTORY (part one)!

The Government pledges funds for every secondary school and college in England, to enable them to offer free period products to all their students.

Free Periods continues to campaign for the pledge to be rolled out in all primary schools, too.

April 2019 – VICTORY (part two)!

The Government commits to make funds available in all primary schools in England.

June 2019

Free Periods starts work on a global campaign to end period poverty in schools.

September 2019

Free Periods launches #FreePeriodsStories, a campaign encouraging people to share funny, awkward, embarrassing, or meaningful period stories on social media, to normalise the conversation around menstruation.

January 2020

The Government scheme offering free period products for all state-funded schools and colleges in England begins, and is rolled out in all primary schools, secondary schools, and colleges.

FURTHER READING

Adan Ismail, Edna and Wendy Holden, *A Woman of Firsts* (London: HQ, 2019).

Adichie, Chimamanda Ngozi, *We Should All Be Feminists* (London: Fourth Estate, 2014).

Angelou, Maya, *And Still I Rise* (London: Virago Press, 2009).

Criado Perez, Caroline, *Invisible Women* (London: Chatto & Windus, 2019).

Curtis, Scarlett, *Feminists Don't Wear Pink (and other lies)* (London: Penguin Books, 2018).

Eddo-Lodge, Reni, *Why I'm No Longer Talking to White People About Race* (London: Bloomsbury Publishing, 2017).

Frances-White, Deborah, *The Guilty Feminist* (London: Virago Press, 2018).

Hirsch, Afua, *Brit(ish)* (London: Vintage, 2018).

Martin, Gina, *Be The Change* (London: Sphere, 2019).

Solnit, Rebecca, *Hope in the Dark* (Edinburgh: Canongate, 2016).

Walker, Sophie, *Five Rules for Rebellion: Let's Change the World Ourselves* (London: Icon Books, 2020).

ACKNOWLEDGEMENTS

Firstly, thank you to the 28 activists who generously shared their stories and wisdom in this book. You've proven that activism can look and feel different to everyone, but will always matter. Thank you for your vulnerability, openness, and your tireless work in making the world a better place.

Thank you to Scarlett and Grace for helping me turn a wild idea into an actual period protest.

Thank you to Gemma, Janvi, and Clegg for your ambition and continual dedication to Free Periods.

Thank you so much to my truly brilliant editors (old and new): Victoria Moynes, Rachel Kenny, and Nira Begum. Thank you to Lisa Milton and the incredible team at HQ for investing in this book with so much passion and optimism.

Thank you to Georgia Garrett, for making this journey easier, for always understanding, and for your kind honesty. Thank you to Honor Spreckley for all your help.

Thank you to Grace, my sister and strength, who will never know how much she means to me and, admittedly, knows me 'better than I know myself'.

Thank you to Meike, who has had to put up with me in various states of stress, and has been my constant support, from across the corridor or across the Atlantic. And thank you to my friends who always know what to say and have stuck by me, even when I don't reply to messages – especially Anna, Grace, Hannah, Maya, Sophie, Ben, Zak, Sam, Alex, Milly, Charlie, Esther and Tiger. And Carys, Hannah, Izzy, Marie, and Tabi, who have been there since the beginning.

Thank you to my *huge* family who believed in me more than I ever did. Ayee, Dada, Ammachi, my uncles and aunties, my Chachas and Chachis, and my cousins – I love you all.

Thank you to my dad, whose humour and integrity inspires everything I do, and my brother, Millan, who I wish I was more like.

And, above all, to my mum, the most thoughtful, determined, ambitious activist I know.

FEATURING INTERVIEWS WITH

Adwoa Aboah

Alice Aedy

Aranya Johar

Bruna Elias

Camryn Garrett

Caroline Criado Perez OBE

Catherine Miller

Deborah Frances-White

Gabby Edlin

Grace Campbell

Gina Martin

Hannah Witton

Inés Yábar

Josie Naughton

Kia Abdullah

Laura Coryton

Maya and Gemma Tutton

Nicola Mendelsohn CBE

Rima Amin

Scarlett Curtis

Seyi Akiwowo

Shiden Tekle

Dr Shola Mos-Shogbamimu

Sophie Cowling

Sophie Walker

Suhaiymah Manzoor-Khan

Tiara Sahar Ataii

Tasha Bishop